Corpses of Unity.
An Anthology of Poems

Cadavres de l'unité.
Une anthologie de poèmes

Edited by / Dirigé par - Nsah Mala & Mbizo Chirasha

Nairobi

Published in 2020.
Vita Books
P.O. Box 62501-00200
Nairobi. Kenya
http://vitabooks.co.uk
info.vitabkske@gmail.com; info@
vitabooks.co.uk

Distributed Worldwide by:
African Books Collective
P.O. Box 721
Oxford, OX1 9EN
orders@africanbookscollective.com
www.africanbookscollective.com

Design & Layout: Kariuki Maina.
petermaina1st@gmail.com

Uni.Way House, Second Floor, University Way
Next to Lilian Towers
P.O. Box 62501-00200
Nairobi, Kenya
info.vitabkske@gmail.com
http://vitabooks.co.uk

CONTENTS – CONTENUS

Préface : 'Untermensch' en colonie et néocolonie camerounaises

S'il y a un concept qui commande une attention particulière, c'est bien 'holocauste/ génocide'. Juifs et pro-juifs se le réclament et prennent ombrage quand on l'applique aux situations similaires. Le plus grand écrivain francophone Aime Césaire avait été toute sa vie mis en situation d'ostracisme parce qu'il avait osé exposer une vision hypocrite bien française. Dans son excellent discours à l'Assemblée française en 1959, il éduque ceux-là mêmes en mettant sur le même pied d'égalité qui colonisent en Afrique et ailleurs comme des Nazis. Colonialisme=Nazisme, démontrait alors le poète Martiniquais lorsqu'il pose cette autre équation ou le barbarisme volontaire participe de la provocation pure et simple à savoir Colonialisme=Chosification.[1] Je vois déjà des sceptiques lâcher bouf, quand ils ouvriront ce recueil de poèmes que Mbizo Chirasha et Nsah Mala ont aidé à sortir pour exposer l'ensauvagement [encore un autre barbarisme du même Césaire dans le même discours] de Southern Cameroons/Ambazonia. Depuis les travaux du Palestinien-Américain Edward Saïd, on a coutume d'entendre des cris lorsqu'on pose la question palestinienne comme génocide. La question bamiléké hier et la question ambazonienne aujourd'hui m'interpellent que je réécrive 'génocide' pour ne pas m'abaisser à prononcer 'holocauste' que le monde judéo-chrétien pratique dans les colonies esclavagistes depuis des siècles. L'histoire retiendra que depuis Novembre 2017, le 'bon tyran' Paul Biya planifie et systématiquement détruit la vie en Ambazonie. Que de jeunes poètes à l'ère des nouvelles technologies décident de crever cet abcès ne peut que susciter l'agacement de ceux qui sont repus du sang des peuples opprimés. Comment choisir le silence ou le bien parler lorsque dans un pays comme le Cameroun il y a des médias comme la chaine de TV Vision 4 qui use des métaphores comme 'rats' et 'deratisation' pour nommer ceux de nos freres et soeurs qui ont pris les armes pour dire non à la mort arbitraire ?

Le poème liminaire de cette collection énonce sans ambiguïté et sans far : « The Holocaust/ came like doomsday ». Est-il ici question d'une simple boursouflure, une inutile inflammation de l'imagination du poète ? Ou est-ce banalisation d'un concept qui ne s'appliquerait qu'à un cas de l'Histoire classique euro-centrique à savoir celui des Juifs ? Je reviens à la souche juive de la France, nation génocidaire, pour qu'on comprenne la nature et le fonctionnement d'un corps génocidaire comme le BIR [Brigade d'Intervention Rapide] créé et formé par un Israélite, et la monstration orgueilleuse des dirigeants français comme Emmanuel Macron. Je tiens à rappeler que cette gangrène est pensée et implantée par ceux-là mêmes qui furent, en partie, sauvés de l'hydre que fut le nazisme. L'ironie, et je le dis en larmes que je verse pour chaque corps qui tombe en Ambazonie, je dis que l'ironie est que ce sont nos ancêtres indigènes qui, véritables ouragans, partirent de l'empire français pour entrainer la Chute de l'Hydre, pour paraphraser le titre d'un ouvrage du poète Louis-Marie Pouka, Hitler ou la chute de l'Hydre (1948). Je convoque Pouka ici pour dire qu'au moment où les Français fauchaient à larges andins dans leurs ambitions impériales, il y en avait parmi les victimes qui pleuraient sur le sort de leur génocideur.

---

1 Aimé Césaire. *Discours sur le colonialisme*. Paris : Présence Africaine, 1959.
2 Jean-Marie Teno (dir). *Le Malentendu colonial*. Les Films de Raphia, 2004.

Depuis que le bon tyran Paul Biya a déclaré la guerre à la minorité du Southern Cameroons aka Ambazonia le 30 novembre 2017, les réseaux sociaux inondent le monde entier du concept génocide. A quel moment des voix soucieuses crient au génocide, lorsqu'une majorité décident de porter atteinte au droit de vie d'une minorité ? Quels mots, quelles phrases d'une majorité belliqueuse traduisent les intentions d'élimination physique et spirituelle de sa minorité pour que le monde sorte de sa torpeur ? Pendant des siècles et non des décennies, l'arrogante Allemagne dite race aryenne, nomma les autres races des 'untermensch' ou 'sous-hommes'. Entre les deux guerres, les juifs furent leur cible principale. L'ultime résultat fut ce que le monde a depuis longtemps déploré, voire réparé, le 'Holocaust juif'. Et pourtant la même Allemagne avait déjà pris les Hereros de la Namibie comme terrain d'expérimentation. C'était au temps des colonies. On sait ce qui en est de cette minorité.[2]

Cette même Allemagne qui orchestra le repas de la partition de l'Afrique à Berlin donnait le feu vert pour un bien plus vaste 'holocauste' dont le sien eu pour terrain entre autres le Kamerun. Cette première phase de génocide fut de fait, mais est-il besoin de revenir sur la deuxième phase, de facto par la France et l'Angleterre ? Donc l'extermination des juifs ne fut nullement le premier acte génocidaire allemande. Avec le colonialisme/nazisme en Afrique ne sommes-nous pas en pleins pieds sur le 'dark continent' ? Les mots, parfois, précèdent les actes et l'on dit 'holocauste' en parole avant que de le faire dans les actes. Les historiens occidentaux, osons le dire, se refusent d'appliquer à l'Afrique le concept qu'il juge juste, à savoir le génocide. Oser nommer chat chat et chien chien c'est emboiter le pas de celui dont les oeuvres devraient servir d'instruments d'éducation, en un mot des classiques au sein des peuples ou les violations des droits humains sont le lot quotidien des « … malheurs qui n'ont point de voix… »[3] Ecrire à propos du Kamerun et de ses dérivés Cameroun/Cameroons, c'est prendre fait et cause pour les victimes du génocidaire d'aujourd'hui et d'hier, car la France traite les Ambazoniens comme elle l'a fait hier des bamilékés. On ne peut séparer les deux crimes contre l'humanité. Ils sont liés parce qu'avant tout pesés, pensés et exécutés par le colonat français et ses zélotes.

Or donc, ce qui se passe en pays bamiléké de 1958 à 1971 ne fut ni plus ni moins qu'un génocide. Le discours, je l'ai démontré ailleurs, précéda les actes. Le colonel Jean Lamberton pose et justifie ainsi qu'il suit l'extermination de cette minorité dont une partie est ambazonienne : « Le Cameroun s'engage sur les chemins de l'indépendance avec, dans sa chaussure un caillou bien gênant. »[4] Pour qui a vécu sous l'artillerie lourde, les bombardements au napalm en pays bamiléké, l'officier français ne fait que confirmer ce qui est fait avant et après l'indépendance du Cameroun français en 1960. Le colonel Jean Lamberton, le General Briand, Roland Pré, Pierre Mesmer sont, pour la plupart d'anciens, maquisards, de véritables tortionnaires de la guerre d'Indochine et l'Algérie. Charles de Gaulle dirige une escouade de criminels tout au long et après la Deuxième Guerre Mondiale ayant pour vocation de coloniser. Comme je le dis clairement en hommage à Edward Saïd, une voix singulière dans une Amérique qui avait plongé ses racines dans l'extermination des minorités indiennes, lorsque vous avez un caillou dans votre chaussure, une seule solution s'offre à vous : l'extraire.[5] Il y a donc entre la France et les communautés bamiléké/amazoniennes une hargne d'extermination qui se transmet de gouvernement en gouvernement, de zélotes franco-camerounais en zélotes camerounais. Faucher à larges andins comme on l'a fait hier comme on le fait aujourd'hui et s'offrir, lit-on dans les réseaux sociaux, un milliard cinq cent millions de beuverie participe d'un luciferisme bien franco-français.

La France étant dans le coup, enfoncée jusqu'à la gorge, que nous reste-t-il sinon dire la vérité crue ? C'était donc avant-hier. J'avais bien opté pour le concept génocide pour dire les horreurs perpétrées en pays bamiléké. Pendant plus d'une décennie, cette région fut transformée en un carré d'océan où les têtes exposées sur les places publiques et les corps flottant dans les cours d'eau offraient un macabre spectacle au Lucifer pour le grand bonheur et la bravoure de jeunes militaires comme Pierre Semengue. On coupait alors les têtes humaines comme on le fait de celles des moutons. La tradition s'est installée avec en sous-main la même France. Hier, aux côtés des Belges la même France armait et instruisait la minorité Hutus. Aux yeux des Hutus du Rwanda, les Tutsis étaient des cancrelats. La radio des 7 collines en fit le refrain du discours officiel de la majorité Hutu au pouvoir. Le monde entier ferma les yeux pour les ouvrir sur le génocide de 1994. Ce même monde offrit l'asile politique aux Hutus. Le Cameroun aussi, car je le dis déjà dans Au-delà du lac de nénuphars.6 Bien nos institutions comme l'ESSTIC ont formé des Hutus, souvent protégés par le régime de Yaoundé. Aujourd'hui, la dérive tribale d'un média au service de régime comme Vision 4 me fait penser aux émissions comme Bebela Ebouk, qui vouait les Anglo-Bami aux feux purificateurs dans les années 1990s. Nous n'avions ni une presse libre alors, ni les réseaux sociaux d'aujourd'hui. Internet, Facebook, Twitter, Instagram, etc., sont devenus la plateforme où le monde entier peut dénoncer la politique de l'autruche, hypocrite et injuste des puissances destructrices comme les anciens empires anglais, français et autres allemands, Hollandais, Belges.

Sous la houlette de deux poètes, l'un du Cameroon [Nsah Mala], et l'autre du Zimbabwe [Mbizo Chirasha], 33 poètes du continent et d'ailleurs dévêtissent la tyrannie qui fauche à larges andins dans l'ancien Southern Cameroons. Si depuis la déclaration de guerres contre les soi-disant terroristes sécessionnistes, des médias comme Vision 4 exhortent, ni plus ni moins, la dératisation les zones anglophones, des voix prennent le contrepied sur les réseaux sociaux pour exposer

l'hécatombe qu'est devenu l'Ambazonie. Prophètes de malheur, ces voix se refusent de chanter quand Rome est en flammes. Elles assument le devoir de leur génération et font écho avec Césaire qui posait, ferme, intransigeant : « Ma bouche sera la bouche des malheurs qui n'ont point de bouche et Voix, la liberté de celles qui s'affaissent au cachot du désespoir. »7 Pouvaient-elles, ces 'Voix', se taire lorsque les langues pendantes aux bouts des têtes décollées comme celle de Florence Ayafor faisaient le tour de la toile ? Comme je l'ai écrit dans La Cicatrice (2013)8, le poète est dans un tel contexte à la fois, la 'Voix' et l'OEil' qui percent l'obscurité la plus épaisse. Mbizo apostrophe le régime vampirique pour lancer ironique aux yeux de la horde enivrée :

> *Cameroon,*
> *You cannot drink your own eggs in the name of expediency.*
> *You cannot slash wombs in daylight and*
> *Let your machetes drink blood of children in dawns of violence.*

Depuis qu'il est au pouvoir, Biya a toujours fermé les yeux sur 'le Problème Anglophone'. Les soubresauts qui accompagnent ses reformes portant sur le nom et le système éducatif connaissent son silence hautain. Comment ne pas voir dans l'interpellation ironique de Mbizo cette arrogance hautaine ? Penser que les « …machetes drink blood of children in dawns of violence », participe des actions qu'on commet dans l'ombre et qu'on croit invisible. Et Nsah Mala de rencherir, « Some dig mass graves in darkness/And fill them with corpses butchered for unity. » Elles rivalisent avec les organisations internationales comme Amnesty International, Human Rights Watch, l'Union Européenne et même des pays comme les USA, dans l'indexation du régime sanguinaire de Yaoundé qui, au nom de l'unité nationale, a fait de l'horreur le quotidien de la minorité anglophone. Parfois en contact avec un frère en fuite dans les brousses, en exil intérieur comme extérieur, ces voix sont informées pour dire. Ainsi, Corpses of Unity se lit comme un testament des faits qui accablent l'autocrate sanguinaire de Yaoundé, qui se refuse de laisser le pouvoir comme Robert Mugabe du Zimbabwe. Une manière de vampire, de squelette ambulant, Biya comme Mugabe ne se rajeunie-t-il pas au côté de sa prostituée de femme ? On peut lire dans le rapport établi par des chercheurs d'Oxford University School of Law :

> *The Report considers evidence of human rights abuses that have been committed by the Cameroonian State forces and by separatist groups in the anglophone regions. Suspected human rights violations include extra-judicial killings, torture, destruction of property, fair trial violations, and inhumane and degrading conditions of detention. These violations breach both Cameroonian national laws and international human rights laws that bind Cameroon.[9]*

Le premier rapport citant des chiffres qui déjà étaient discutables c'est le cas d'International Crisis Group qui dans la synthèse de son report No. 272, publié le 4 mai 2019, énonçait : « Au Cameroun, la crise anglophone s'est embourbée. Après vingt mois d'affrontements, 1 850 morts, 530 000 déplacés internes et des dizaines de milliers de réfugiés, le pouvoir et les séparatistes campent sur des positions inconciliables. »[10] Exaspérés par l'arrogance du tyranneau de Yaoundé qui a le soutien du président français Emmanuel Macron, les USA viennent de frapper Yaoundé en décrétant des sanctions économiques contre le Cameroun. Ce qui taraude les américains, c'est l'insensibilité de Biya face à la tragédie

---

3 Aimé Césaire. La Tragédie du Roi Christophe. Paris : Présence Africaine, 1963.

4 Journal Officiel de la Défense, 1960, (C'est moi qui souligne).

5 Gilbert Doho. « Subject and Citizen : Ambivalent Identity in Postcolonial Cameroon », in Paradoxical Citizenship : Essays on Edward Saïd. New York : Lexington Books, 2006, pp. 175-185.

6 Gilbert Doho. Au-delà du lac de nénuphars. Ottawa : Editions Malaika, 2004.

7 Aimé Césaire. Cahier d'un retour au pays natal. Paris : Présence, Africaine, 1939.

8 Gilbert Doho. La Cicatrice. New Jersey : Africa World Press, 2013.

9 Voir Oxford University, <https://ohrh.law.ox.ac.uk/wordpress/wp-content/uploads/2019/11/Cameroon-Anglophone-Crisis-Report-online.pdf>

10 Voir International Crisis Group, <https://www.crisisgroup.org/fr/africa/central-africa/cameroon/272-crise-anglophone-au-cameroun-comment-arriver-aux-pourparlers>

qu'il peut arrêter, comme il a commencé. Le Diplomate américain avait été très clair lors de sa visite au Cameroun. Donner une photo où Biya est avec George Bush père, constitue une puissante métaphore à un vieillard de 86 ans qui tyrannise son pays depuis près de quarante ans. Le problème véritable du Cameroun c'était un vieillard insensible aux misères de son peuple. Car une excessive usure au pouvoir conduit à l'improductivité que connait le Cameroun aujourd'hui. Car de George Bush père à Donald Trump, Paul Biya a vu de défiler à la Maison Blanche pas moins de cinq présidents démocratiquement élus. Tout sourire, le tyranneau n'a rien compris.

De la diplomatie de velours, les Américains viennent de passer à celle du marteau. C'est ainsi que le Président Donald Trump vient de signifier au Congres dans une lettre d'information qu'il a pris un Executive Order de suspendre le Cameroun d'un programme vital à ce pays pauvre et extrêmement endetté :

In accordance with section 506A(a)(3)(B) of the Trade Act of 1974, as amended (19 U.S.C. 2466a(a)(3)(B)), I am providing notice of my intent to terminate the designation of the Republic of Cameroon (Cameroon) as a beneficiary sub-Saharan African country under the African Growth and Opportunity Act (AGOA).[11]

A la suite de cette exclusion du Cameroun de l'AGOA, les USA s'est retrouvées dans la situation d'avouer au monde entier l'ampleur de la tragédie que Biya en fin de règne écrit au Cameroun. Qu'un diplomate comme Tibor Nagy se risque à avancer le chiffre de 12.000 morts en Ambazonie n'est pas un fait du hazard. Il confirme ce que par anticipation le poète avait déjà vu en titrant cette collection Corpses of Unity. Et pour mémoire je cite ci-dessous la Une d'un journal proche de la tyrannie de Yaoundé :

---

11 Voir AGOA INFO, <https://agoa.info/news/article/15683-agoa-eligibility-of-cameroon-message-to-congress-by-the-white-house.html>

Prophètes de Bonheur

Terminer en larmes ? Que non ! Le poète n'est pas un inutile encombrement de l'espace social. Il faut être hypocrite comme Malherbe pour chanter les louanges des monarques en vers et déclarer : « Un poète n'est pas plus utile à la société qu'un bon joueur de quilles. » Historien à sa manière, le poète utilise le passé pour pointer la voie du futur à sa génération. Et Nancy Ndeke d'interpeler non le loqueteux Biya, véritable cadavre ambulant à la tête du Cameroun, mais la génération présente et à venir :

> *O Cameroon,*
> *Haven't you seen the bloodied brothers?*
> *In Rwanda,*
> *In South Sudan,*

Prophètes de Bonheur

Terminer en larmes ? Que non ! Le poète n'est pas un inutile encombrement de l'espace social. Il faut être hypocrite comme Malherbe pour chanter les louanges des monarques en vers et déclarer : « Un poète n'est pas plus utile à la société qu'un bon joueur de quilles. » Historien à sa manière, le poète utilise le passé pour pointer la voie du futur à sa génération. Et Nancy Ndeke d'interpeler non le loqueteux Biya, véritable cadavre ambulant à la tête du Cameroun, mais la génération présente et à venir :

> *O Cameroon,*
> *Haven't you seen the bloodied brothers?*
> *In Rwanda,*
> *In South Sudan,*
> *And learnt the outcomes,*
> *That talking keeps at bay bloodletting?*

En d'autres termes, Corpses of Unity constitue la 'Voix' du continent que Mbizo et Mala unie pour exorciser, en d'autres termes, guérir et prévenir. Anthologie de la poétique de guerre, cette collection est la revanche de la vie sur le mort, un devoir de mémoire pour ceux qui sont morts sans parler. Elle est comme je l'ai dit plus haut, OEil d'Abel brulant sur le front génocidaire de la coterie de Yaoundé qui aujourd'hui noce quand des corps jonchent Ambaland. Tout poète est aussi messager de paix et d'espoir car être c'est aller au rythme de la vie et de la mort. Le poète est donc la vie qui se rit de la mort et énonce comme le fait Ayouba Toure dans le poème terminal :

> *I prayed serenity will come like a new-born baby*
> *Just like a rain,*
> *It shall pour its droplets on every thatch hut in our village, Cameroon.*

Mais faut-il s'en remettre à la prière ? Combien nos frères anglophones en ont offert à un Dieu sourd qui là-haut s'occupe de ses affaires ? Dans un pays où l'élimination physique des religieux est devenue un sport national depuis les années 1980s, faut-il encore s'en remettre à une puissance divine ? Sans être adepte de la violence, il faut bien reconnaitre que le courage de nombreux Ambazoniens, jeunes, âgés, hommes, femmes, bref des Ambaboys, a permis au monde de Voir et de Dire. On crache en l'air pour avoir le mucus sur son nez et non celui des autres. Que le régime génocidaire de Yaoundé apprenne cette leçon que Corpses of Unity codifie pour les générations de demain. On meure debout quand un cadavre ambulant vous tient à la gorge, sans remords.

Gilbert Doho est poète, dramaturge, romancier et essayiste. Il enseigne les langues et littératures francophones à Case Western Reserve University.

Editors' Note

Scattered Unity

2012
Five days past May's Ides!
Fifty or fifty-one old we are.
Two Satans have lorded over us;
The last one says our porous Union is 40.
Last Satan is worst; he has clocked 30.
See his black-, red-, and green-capped
Wasps filing past the Boulevard!
All our coins go to procure their long flashy cars,
Bullets and canons. The King' secured!

Mokolo
Same day! Nursing moms, old dames, grey-headed dads
And futureless youths bask the sun like agamas;
They brave the rains and drink mud like fish,
Just to exist. They can't live. Will Ntimi
Turn up in the morrow? They wonder and ponder.
Unity Day, they say it is. Cat-mice unity?
Ngu Foncha alone can tell.

Elsewhere
Every time! Teacherless classrooms and nurseless
Health centres. Always too indebted we are.
Roadless interiors in perpetual darkness.
State liars and thieves only come in December
To sing Satan's hymns and preach disjointed unity.
Day-night unity?
Tandeng Muna alone can tell.

– Nsah Mala, Chaining Freedom, 2012, p. 55

When co-editor Nsah Mala penned and published the above poem in 2012, the cracks on the collapsing walls of Cameroon's unity were not yet visible to everybody. But writers, as they say, are prophets. That is why he was able to discern the cracks at that time, standing on the shoulders of earlier Anglophone Cameroonian literary prophets such as Bernard Fonlon, Bate Besong, Bole Butake, John Nkemngong Nkengasong, and Victor Epie'Ngome, among others. As usual, irresponsible rulership, especially in Africa, always chooses to ignore and/or molest writer-prophets instead of heeding their warnings in order to mitigate impending dangers. Par conséquent, le Cameroun est en train de descendre en cendres aujourd'hui. Cameroon is fighting a dirty war with herself. Mais, pourquoi ?

Cameroon has refused to reconcile herself to her complicated and complex history. D'abord, le Cameroun n'existe pas, comme tout autre pays en Afrique. Ce que nous appelons les pays en Afrique sont tous des inventions coloniales. This brings us to the European imperial invention of what is called Cameroon/Cameroun today. Despite initial British influence along the coast of Cameroon through Baptist Missionary activities led by Joseph Merrick, Joseph Jackson Fuller, and Alfred Saker around Bimbia and Victoria

(Limbe), Germany finally signed an annexation treaty with two Douala Kings in 1884 and forcibly expanded into the hinterlands to create the German colony of Kamerun. When a combined Franco-British force defeated the Germans in Kamerun in 1916 during WWI, the colony was partitioned between Britain and France. The Oliphant-Picot Demarcation Line of 1916 offered about three-fifths of Cameroon to France and about two-fifths to Britain. In 1922 the League of Nations officially conferred the two parts as Mandated Territories to France and Britain which became known as the British Cameroons and French Cameroun, respectively. For the ease of colonial administration Britain administered her part jointly with her colony of Nigeria while France maintained hers as a separate part of French Equatorial Africa. After WWII, the two parts evolved to the status of UN Trusteeship Territories still under the control of Britain and France. On 1st January 1960 French Cameroun obtained "independence" from France and became the Republic of Cameroun. On 11th February 1961 a UN-organized Plebiscite compelled British Cameroons to choose to obtain independence by joining either the Federal Republic of Nigeria (which gained independence in 1960) or the Republic of Cameroun. The British Northern Cameroons voted to join Nigeria while the British Southern Cameroons voted to join French Cameroun in a Federation. On 1st October 1961 British Southern Cameroons achieved independence by joining the Republic of Cameroun to form the Federal Republic of Cameroon, with English and French as two official languages, equal in status.

According to the Foumban Constitution, the Federal Republic of Cameroon consisted of two states equal in status: the State of East Cameroon (former Republic of Cameroun) and the State of West Cameroon (former British Southern Cameroons). The French civil law and educational system were to be applied in East Cameroon while the Anglo-Saxon common law and educational system were to be practiced in West Cameroon. And there was a constitutional clause prohibiting any eventual dissolution of the Federation. Despite this prohibition, Cameroun's first president Ahmadou Ahidjo (a Francophone) dissolved the Federation on 20th May 1972 through a controversial "referendum" and created the United Republic of Cameroon, consequently breeding the principal root cause of the Anglophone Problem which has culminated in the genocidal war ravaging Anglophone Cameroon (former Southern Cameroons) today. Depuis 1972, les anglophones se sont sentis marginalisés et discriminés au Cameroun avec plus de pouvoir exercé par les francophones. Pour empirer les choses, Cameroon's second president Paul Biya (another Francophone who was handed power in 1982 and is still in office) single-handedly changed the country's name from the United Republic of Cameroon to the Republic of Cameroun, the original name of French Cameroun at independence, before the 1961 Federation. This gesture of bad faith further infuriated Anglophone Cameroonians. As a result, Southern Cameroonian lawyer and political activist Fongum Gorji-Dinka declared on 20th March 1985 that French Cameroun had pulled out of the 1961 union with Southern Cameroons and Southern Cameroons would henceforth be called Ambazonia, coined from the Ambas Bay in Victoria (Limbe). This laid the groundwork for a separatist movement called the Southern Cameroons National Council (SCNC) which emerged in the 1990s advocating for the restoration of the 1961 Independence of the British Southern Cameroons. The SCNC gained relatively more support from some former Social Democratic Front (SDF) militants in the two Anglophone regions (then provinces) of Northwest and Southwest who were disgruntled with the 1992 electoral fraud that prevented Ni John Fru Ndi (the Anglophone founding chairman of the SDF) from becoming President in Cameroon. Un anglophone voulait devenir Président au Cameroun ? Pas possible, disaient les autres ! D'aucuns appelaient Fru Ndi et ses militants anglophones "les Biafrais" recrutés pour destabiliser le Cameroun !

While Anglophone Cameroonians continued to face different forms of marginalization and assimilation including exclusion from key political positions (despite the ceremonial position of Prime Minister since 1992) and the gradual erosion of their Anglo-Saxon educational and judiciary systems through dubious policies such as harmonization and national integration, there was however minimal support for the separatist SCNC movement among the Anglophone Cameroonian population until recently. In fact, following the continuous deployment of French-speaking teachers to teach English subjects in Anglophone schools and French-speaking judges without mastery of common law to preside over Anglophone courts, Anglophone Cameroonian teachers' and lawyers' syndicates launched a series of peaceful demonstrations in late 2016 demanding the Yaoundé government to stop eroding their systems. The strikes brought schools to a close. Uniformed officers on instructions from Yaoundé began brutalizing the peaceful demonstrators. The Anglophone Cameroonian population joined the striking unionists in demanding a return to the original two-state Federation as the only way to protect the Anglophone minority status and stop further assimilation and marginalization from the Francophone ruling elite. From a mix of denying the existence of an Anglophone Problem and the adoption of some cosmetic measures to quell the protests to more repression and brutalization including uniformed persons firing live ammunition at peaceful demonstrators and massive arrests of unionists and protesters, the Yaoundé regime only succeeded to prolong the crisis and to radicalize some Anglophones, thereby pushing them towards a separatist ideology. On 1st October 2017, there was a massive turnout of peaceful Anglophone protesters who chanted songs and proclaimed the restoration of the 1961 Independence of the British Southern Cameroons into a new country christened the Federal Republic of Ambazonia. That resulted in more brutality and killings orchestrated by uniformed officers on instructions from Yaoundé. Consequently, some young Anglophone men and women took up Dane guns and other rudimentary weapons to defend their communities against military brutality thereby sporadically killing a few uniformed officers. In response, Paul Biya officially declared war against what he initially termed « une bande de terroristes se réclamant d'un mouvement sécessionniste » on 30 November 2017 and the crisis quickly morphed into a full-blown armed conflict.

It must be noted that killing, brutalizing, and arresting Anglophones only helped to radicalize more Anglophones both at home and abroad. For instance, in early 2017 after the Yaoundé regime surprisingly arrested the Anglophone unionist leaders with whom the government had been holding fruitless talks, the leadership of the Anglophone revolution was taken over by some Anglophone Cameroonian activists abroad, especially in Nigeria, South Africa, Europe, and North America. The diaspora activists are mostly made up of marginalized Anglophone youth who have grim experiences with the Francophone dictatorship back home. They designated Julius Sisiku Ayuk Tabe (then based in Nigeria) as the President of the Interim Government of Ambazonia, but Ayuk Tabe was arrested with 46 other separatist leaders in a hotel in Abuja, Nigeria's capital, forcibly and illegally extradited to Yaoundé in January 2018 and held incommunicado for many months. Some of the leaders abducted with Ayuk Tabe included Cornelius Kwanga, Egbe Orock, Eyambe Ebai, Fidelis Nde Che, Kimeng Henry, Nfor Ngala Nfor, Augustine Awasum, Shufai Blaise, and Tassang Wilfred, among others, most of whom were refugees and asylum seekers. Although a Nigerian court ruled in March 2018 that their arrest and extradition were illegal, a Cameroonian military tribunal went ahead to sentence them to life imprisonment in August 2019, further aggravating the conflict. Despite infighting and the existence of many fractions within them, Anglophone diaspora activists continue to play a crucial role in the crisis. For example, they raise funds to help arm separatists on Ground Zero (back home), demonstrate(d) in front of UN offices and strategic diplomatic missions in their host countries, and engage in international lobbying. As a result, they have successfully brought more intentional attention to the war (especially consistent pressure from Washington on Yaoundé and separatists to genuinely tackle the root causes of the conflict in an inclusive dialogue without preconditions with a view to a possible reinstitution of the 1961 federal system) and they are willing to engage in mediation (dialogue) with Yaoundé in a safe and credible process like the one offered by Switzerland, despite reluctance/refusal from Yaoundé. Avec le soutien constant de Paris, Yaoundé n'a pas peur, on dirait ! Ainsi la guerre ne fait que continuer ! Anglophones are material for death!

By December 2019, international human rights NGOs estimated that more than 12000 people had died in the war while regular soldiers had razed down over 400 villages and partially burnt down some hospitals. Separatist fighters had attacked some schools, kidnapped some students for disrespecting school boycotts and a few politicians loyal to Yaoundé, and burnt down the homes and businesses of some of such politicians. Government sources indicated that over 700 soldiers had died in the war. International humanitarian NGOs and UN agencies also reported that there were thousands of children out of school, over 50,000 Anglophone Cameroonian refugees in neighbouring Nigeria, and thousands of internally displaced persons (IDPs) within Cameroon, some of whom are taking shelter in forests in all weather, among many other consequences. In June 2019, Jan Egeland, the Secretary General of the Norwegian Refugee Council (NRC) described the conflict as "the world's most neglected crisis," after visiting Anglophone Cameroon. In December 2019, the UN Office for the Coordination of Humanitarian Affairs (OCHA) reported that there were 922 thousand IDPs in Cameroon as a result of the Anglophone conflict, adding that "#Cameroon at 41% remains the most underfunded humanitarian response in Africa."

The international community, especially the United Nations, is apparently helpless in the face of this bloody conflict which resulted from a poorly managed decolonization. All calls for an inclusive dialogue without preconditions to address the root causes of the conflict have been ignored by the Yaoundé government. Instead, the government organized what they called a Grand National Dialogue (which many variously described as Die-Logue, Biya-Logue, or Monologue) from 30th September-4th October 2019 without releasing all detained Anglophones and separatist leaders to engage them in addressing the root cause of the conflict which is undoubtedly the 1972 illegal dissolution of the Cameroon Federation. Having avoided the drafting of a real Constitution to restore the two-state Federation, Cameroon's CPDM ruling party of Paul Biya rather imposed what they call a "Special Status" on the Anglophone regions in respect of their policy of decentralization which was adopted in a 1996 constitution and was never implemented. Comme Paris soutient le soit-disant Statut Spécial, Yaoundé se sent rassuré et ne veut donc pas entreprendre un vrai dialogue inclusif avec les leaders Ambazoniens. Yaoundé refuse de prendre part à l'initiative de médiation proposée par la Suisse pour chercher les voies de sortie de cette crise. N'est-ce pas Paris promet de l'argent pour reconstruire les villages anglophones incendiés par l'armée sans que Yaoundé ne déclare un cessez-le-feu ? Comment peut-on recontruire en pleine guerre ? Pourtant, le 12 novembre 2019 lors du Forum sur la Paix tenu à Paris Paul Biya a finalement et ouvertement avoué le projet échoué qui visait l'assimilation des anglophones au Cameroun, mais ne veut toujours pas s'attaquer aux véritables causes de la guerre actuelle. Entre temps, casualties continue to rise every second, further reducing chances of ending the conflict. More corpses continue to fall for Cameroon's unity to rise!

In the face of this impasse, we have chosen to join our literary voices to the international calls for genuine and inclusive dialogue or mediation, justice, healing, and peace in Cameroon. Given that art and literature are indispensable, harmless weapons capable of ending wars and protecting humanity, a number of single-authored and edited literary anthologies have been published or are forthcoming on the dirty war in Anglophone Cameroon. So far, most if not all of the anthologies have focused either on Anglophone Cameroonian writers or both Anglophone and Francophone Cameroonian writers, thereby excluding writers from other parts of Africa and the world. Simultaneously complementing these publications and also diverging from them, the present anthology, entitled Corpses of Unity – Cadavres de l'Unité, has been edited by Nsah Mala from Anglophone or West Cameroon (former British Southern Cameroons) and Mbizo Chirasha from Zimbabwe. Building on a mini-anthology entitled Blood Letters to Biya: Cameroon Is Also Our Country which co-editor Mbizo Chirasha curated and published on the Cameroonian situation in December 2018 on his blog Miombo Publishing, the present anthology welcomed contributions from Cameroonians, Africans and other global citizens who are concerned with the blood baths, burnings and other crimes committed in Anglophone Cameroon in the name of unity or division. With entries in English and French, this anthology contains sixty-four (64) poems from thirty-three (33) poets representing thirteen (13) countries viz. Cameroon, Comoros Islands, Congo-Brazzaville, Côte d'Ivoire, Kenya, Malawi, Nigeria, Liberia, Pakistan, Sierra Leone, South Africa, Uganda, and Zimbabwe. Counting forty-one (41) poems in English et vingt-trois (23) textes en français, cette anthologie represents Cameroon's bilingual nature while revealing an interesting irony – the domination of English contributions over French contributions reflects the real positions of English and French in the world today whereas minority English speakers in Cameroon are marginalized and killed! Par cette observation, however, we do not seek to promote linguistic or cultural domination in any part of the world. Difference and diversity mixed with justice, love, equality, and peace constitute key ingredients for the world's beauty, we believe.

The poems in this anthology are both stylistically and thematically striking. The poems paint raw images of the cruel killings of adults, the old and children. They excavate the hidden mass graves and unveil the countless villages reduced to ashes and rubble. They trace the domestic animals fired and burned to waste along with food while immortalizing nurses, patients and teachers brutally killed. Their stanzas meander along with refugees in forests into Nigeria, into the jungles of Mexico en route to the US, and elsewhere. The poems seek to expose the politics of oil and the hypocrisy of international institutions and nations draped in diplomatic garments. It is poetry which speaks for human life and dignity, for peace and education, for dialogue, for reconciliation, while shaming hypocrisy, lip-service efforts, and window dressing au lieu d'un vrai dialogue. It is poetry which ruffles the consciences of those doing business in war, those pulling strings behind curtains, those who see oil before humans, those who trigger guns at their own brothers and sisters and parents, those who give orders to kill – in short, those who enjoy warfare.

While some of the poets may not completely master Cameroon's complicated history and the root causes of the war, they are all quite aware of its devastating consequences, especially on the innocent civilians caught up in between the warring camps. In their poems, some poets seem to gravitate towards freedom for the former British Southern Cameroons aka Ambazonia, some towards Pan-Africanism, and some others towards a reconciled Cameroon. But they all converge on the despicable and gruesome effects of the war on innocent VICTIMS. They all acknowledge that Cameroon is dancing foreignness with bare feet on the dusty soils of her ancestral backyards. There is unanimity among the poets that we Africans hardly question the sources of the belligerence and bellicose adoption of the glitter of otherness fronted at our front doors; so we often jump with one accord to embrace setting-sun values, taking instructions from colonial metropolis to subjugate and maim our own siblings as foreigners cart away our oils and butcher our trees. Ainsi les cadavres ne cessent de tomber au Cameroun pour nourrir son unité. Oui, les cadavres ne cessent d'inonder les rues anglophones afin que la SONARA puisse aroser Paris. Yes, corpses are piling up on Anglophone streets for and against Cameroon's unity. What will become of a "one and indivisible Cameroun" emptied of Anglophones? Petrol will vote. Where did the Federation go to? It disappeared so that Yaoundé should remind Buea not to visit London even though Yaoundé dances Parisian music. In the name of unity stemming from a certain German Kamerun, Yaoundé kills Buea for smiling to London but Yaoundé never hides her Jacobin smiles. Yaoundé cannot forget Paris and join Buea to visit Berlin. And corpses continue to fertilize unity. Even unity is dying, unity is becoming a corpse! A Referendum is both a graveyard and maternity ward! But genuine and inclusive dialoguing can still turn the tides and make Cameroon beautiful again. Yes, genuine and inclusive dialogue can stop more bloodbaths and deaths as we bury the littered Anglophone corpses in a gesture of reconciliation!

– Nsah Mala & Mbizo Chirasha

Publisher's Perspective

Joining hands to liberate Africa, Vita Books is pleased to publish this anthology of poems as a way of fulfilling its aim of 'supporting people's struggles to create societies based on the principles of equality and justice.' At the same time, it meets another of Vita Books' aims — that of 'redressing working people's lack of power over information, communication and the media which then restricts their access to ideas and experiences to resist imperialism'. It is such lack of access that leads to a situation where incidents such as the one below goes unmentioned or get insufficient attention from corporate media, busy with its twin jobs of maximising profits and creating mindsets favourable to capitalism and imperialism:

> The massacres continue to increase in Anglophone Cameroon; it is reported that two days ago, on 14 February 2020, Cameroon government soldiers killed and burnt about thirty people (including children, women and the elderly) taking shelter in their houses in one locality called Ngarbuh (Nsah Mala, personal communications, 16-02-20).

Media sources such as BBC, Crux News, Jeune Afrique, and Modern Ghana (including Wikipedia) also carried the Ngarbuh Massacre. A similar situation was faced by the people of Kenya under the presidency of KANU's Daniel arap Moi (1978-2002). Facing media silence on the massacres and murders by Moi, Kenya resistance activists, organised as Mwakenya and its affiliate, Umoja, published Moi's Reign of Terror in London in 1989. This thoroughly researched document gave details of massacres, murders, jailing and other crimes of the government, and alerted the international community to the atrocities committed by Moi. Hopefully, something similar will happen in the current situation in Cameroon with the publication of this and other books.

With the publication of this book, Vita Books continues to meet new challenges. Since its return to Kenya from exile in London, in 2017, Vita Books has diversified its activities. The first point of departure was to address the language issue. Its first publication in Kenya was the dual language book *Liberating Minds* in English and Gujarati. *Corpses of Unity – Cadavres de l'unité* continues this tradition by publishing in English and French. Later this year we will publish *Tunakataa!* (We Say No), resistance poems from the Moi era, in English and Kiswahili.

In late 2019, Vita Books took another step in meeting its aims by publishing the first issue of the journal The Kenya Socialist. Vita Books thus branched out from book publishing to journals. In addition, it challenged the current publishing ethos by making it available free of charge for download on its website. This indeed was a challenge to capitalism, as was the very subject – socialism. Even the mention of the term 'socialism' has not been allowed in Kenya since the murder of Pio Gama Pinto in 1965 and the banning of the Kenya People's Union in 1969. The publication was hailed as a 'significant step forward for Kenya socialists' by the Communist Review.

Later this year (2020), Vita Books will venture into publications for children and young people with two titles. Similarly, other subjects that Vita Books addresses are class and gender issues in books as well in its journal.

All these issues are not unrelated to the publishing of Corpses of Unity – Cadavres de l'unité. They relate directly to the anti-imperialist struggles in Africa. Imperialism has attacked Africa in multiple ways. It is the military aspect that is prominent and has, rightfully, been the focus. Yet its looting of Africa's resources has been achieved through a carefully planned and executed programme to divide Africa and Africans in as many artificial divisions as possible. The first stage was to divide people and territories into countries without regard to people and their lives and needs just because it suited imperialist interests. But resistance from Africans was so intense that even that was not enough for imperialism to have its way. Other divisions had to be imposed — by class, language, religion, age, gender, ability, among others. In order for Africa to regain its sovereignty, it will have to challenge all these artificially created divisions which serve imperialist aims and go against the interest of African working people. The first battle Africa faces is to liberate its mind from a capitalist and imperialist mindset that imperialism has plunged it into Africa needs to accept class divisions as the key dividing factor, raise class consciousness among people and snatch power from those from their own countries who take the capitalist road and support imperialism. Such a journey is long and requires appropriate ideologies, organisation and leadership. The search for these starts by liberating information and allowing a free flow of alternative, socialist ideas and experiences.

It is here that activities such as those of Vita Books and many others can play a role in the liberation of Africa. The first steps are already being taken. As Nsah Mala mentions in another context, 'the joint publication of the book by different publishers in Africa is another indication of anti-imperialist Pan Africanism which highlights the coming together of African progressive forces.' In this long struggle, Vita Books plays a relatively small part. The hope is that, again to quote Nsah Mala, 'we really wish that this book becomes available as soon as your resources and timeline permit so it can help in raising more awareness on this underreported genocidal war in Anglophone Cameroon.' But we are not alone in this struggle, as increasing numbers of African people resist capitalism and imperialism on a daily basis. As far as this book is concerned, the coming together of so many poets from so many countries is in itself a significant development. It indicates that there are many committed writers with a humanistic perspective who are ready to raise their voices about the sad situation in Cameroon. As the Editors' Note records,

While some of the poets may not completely master Cameroon's complicated history and the root causes of the war, they are all quite aware of its devastating consequences, especially on the innocent civilians caught up in between the warring camps. In their poems, some poets seem to gravitate towards freedom for the former British Southern Cameroons aka Ambazonia, some towards Pan-Africanism, and some others towards a reconciled Cameroon. But they all converge on the despicable and gruesome effects of the war on innocent VICTIMS. They all acknowledge that Cameroon is dancing foreignness with bare feet on the dusty soils of her ancestral backyards. There is unanimity among the poets that we Africans hardly question the sources of the belligerence and bellicose adoption of the glitter of otherness fronted at our front doors; so we often jump with one accord to embrace setting-sun values, taking instructions from colonial metropolis to subjugate and maim our own siblings as foreigners cart away our oils and butcher our trees.

Vita Books applauds the efforts of the thirty-three poets from thirteen countries who have come together to create this anthology. We appreciate the efforts of the Editors in undertaking this major endeavour. This coming together of people from different countries and continents to express their solidarity to the Cameroonian victims is the first necessary step in liberation. Vita Books hopes that the sentiments and contributions of the many poets in this book will also influence the Conference of former African Heads of States on the Southern/Anglophone Cameroonian War to be held in Kenya in April 2020. In this way activism, literature, politics and publishing can come together to help solve the terrible reality that is facing people in Anglophone Cameroon. As Nsah Mala says, 'We stress the activist dimension of the collection as a contribution towards justice and peace in Cameroon.' And we may add, in Africa and the world as a whole. Vita Books joins hands with these poet-activists in this necessary step to African liberation.

I write this on the day in 1952 that colonialists and imperialism assassinated Dedan Kimathi, the leader of Mau Mau. Kenyan activists are marking the day with various events to remember Kimathi and learn the lessons of Mau Mau. Let these poems highlight the need to respect the right to life, equality, peace and justice in Cameroon — and in Africa as a whole.

Shiraz Durrani
Vita Books

The Price of War

Prince Wogu Richardson Eyong

The Holocaust
came like doomsday
to render injustice
for voicing out our plight.
This is the price we pay on Ground Zero.

It's the wedlock of our marriage.
Oh, it's our painful reality!
Flying from machine guns,
thunderous bullets herald our dawn
to usher the speedy violence
designed for our alienation.
This is the fate of our mutiny!
It's the price of war we pay.
Oh, it's our dark reality!

Boys and girls alike sentenced in bloodbath,
their dreams cut short like Martha's.
The future of others looms in dark clouds.
What remedy for their education?
This is the price of ignorance.
Oh, it's our dreaded reality!
Houses and belongings raided by evil fire.
We are indeed homeless in our homeland.
Mothers and fathers alike wander like outcasts
to sooth their pains in nature's warmth
and the world smiles in negligence.
This is the price of Eden's disappointment.
Oh, the gruesome reality of a bitter war!

Sinners in the Hands of Sinners

MD Mbutoh

The killing field belongs to those who have lost their testicles.
Humming machine guns stuttering in the silent forests,
Weeping of running stems in the hands of lumber saws
In the depreciating terrains of Manyu forest and the plains of Ndop.

Hang petals of blood on every eave and
Let the Sinners rise not against the sinner and his hangmen,
For we are all sinners yoked in the unholy alliance
Of adultery, mirthfully bending the 6th Commandment.

In Southern Cameroons, it is Sinners in the hands of Sinners.
The minority Anglophones are Maize in the teeth of a mill crusher,
And petals of blood drizzle in the harvesting fields of Bamenda and Buea.
This is the woe for which the flame must sink into
The leaking bowels of the ocean of blood that floods the land.

The minority bodies are numbed to the incestuous rape by now,
So, the fight is moved to Souls raping in the backyards of sinners.
Bodies trapped in the delicate boulders of the silent Mongolo,
Mutilated body parts swimming gradually into the Atlantic,
And messenger birds lobby and placate lips at the World House of Peace.
The foulest Murder in stark Daylight—before the world's blindness!
When thieves stole sweats and took away minority dreams at their prime,
We shouted and booed as the kite picked the chicks—and keeps picking,
Our curses fly after an escaping kite with our chicks—but the crying
Has been for long & our voices are coarse now yet the kite fires up more…

Our shoots are cut at noon and stems plucked from
The scrotum of dark rich earth, the commander sings praises to
The perfection of his lances.
The hangmen wear garlands and receive pins of honour and ululation
Rain down their valour and fidelity to tyranny and rapists of democracy.

When ticks ache their way into immature flesh
And desecrate the essence of life, murderers walk
Free like the air that pushed down a wall on infants.
Its media covers its dung and the national mic master fans perfume
Over its stench as its curls within the triangle of the Anglophone zone.

It is murder in daylight and confetti of blood rain to reciprocate
the festivity of departing feet.
Graves were once empty stores for a while, but beware of History!
History does not forgive the blunders of youth;
Though mutilated by selfish greenery, History got no pity for innocence!

They were pushed to sit and see; they were made to know that there was a
Powerfuller man who called the shots and Anglophone minority bones
Cackled! History shall have it that the world was blind to the terrorising
Mission upon the Southern Cameroons, and lips mute over identity crime.
My friend, you don't ask to be born—parentage is never the baby's fault.

How nice is it for lost souls to kiss dry feet! A headmaster ruled with a hatchet
And sold the souls of a people on a bed of 61 meadows—petals of blood!
History's wound would heal well, if we use balm of truth and frankness;
For History got no patience, with loops and selfishness!
The baby was too young when sent to lock up with adults on the wine table.

Though the minority bears the brunt of a merciless enemy once seen as comrade,
The weak speak with brutality and violence, and history mocks the likes of
demagogy,
And hails the unflinching stance of truth! Petals of blood ov'r twisters of verity
May pass for the one thing needful now, but History shall bring out the third
Holocaust and Genocide that took place in the era of info and social media!

la saison des armes

Géraldin Mpesse

le temps qui passe ne s'inquiète
point de la douleur qui s'ancre dans le peuple
il l'étouffe en douceur, sans sanglots
et la tragique histoire se griffonne
sur des feuilles volantes

nous sommes les fils de la saison des armes
et nous grandissons dans les rues de l'horreur
où l'aubade matinale des coqs et perdrix
s'éteint dans le tintamarre des rafales
**

ça fait des lustres que le bruit des armes
étouffe les cris des innocents
dont le feu a léché des demeures

ça fait des ans que nous chantons l'hymne
de la paix mais une voix
une voix inconnue tel un muezzin
appelle à la haine

Things They All Do

Nsah Mala

Some dig mass graves in darkness
And fill them with corpses butchered for unity
Because inclusive dialogue is so expensive
And war is so cheap! Who cares to count black corpses?
Rubble and ashes don't speak, they think.
If no camera catches us pants down, we have won.
But rubble and ashes do scream
In the nightmares of culprits
And will surely scream from the walls of their tombs
When they cross the bar.

Some rape and mutilate and chop off hands & heads
In the name of freedom and the struggle
Because in times of war there is no room for opposition
Or divergence of opinions. A black leg is not white.
War, they think, is a fire that burns out all innocence.
But you cannot climb up the mountain to seek freedom
And destroy those for whom you want it,
Except that liberated deserts are trophies for you.
While others bury the unity they need,
You also entomb the freedom you need.

Soon, we may have only emptiness sprouting
To fill the hollow corpses they've littered
For both unity and division while arms dealers
And petrol suitors clang champagne glasses
In celebration of their gains as we scream in pains,
Having evacuated the land of togetherness and separation.
Don't tell me that inclusive dialogue is expensive!

—Aarhus, 17 September 2019

Will of Suppression

Samuella Conteh

A mother's wailing voice rang
across the Sahara and beyond
Echoing pain that is worse than
pangs of childbirth
To see one of her own wielding
whims of hate like an evil twin
of bygone era

Sons separated at birth and flung
Into the harsh world of foster care
While the mother breaths
Refuse to see the other as equal
But dare celebrate coming off age

French brother still sucks on bile
spat in his mouth in oppression
Still high on dope of colonization
he wields the will of suppression
bequeathed to him in fosterhood

His mind's still fettered in slavery
So, he hurts his own sibling
feigning superiority over his brother,
hurling his kith,
howling into forests
and foreign fields

His image is enslaved
like his oppressed brother
and his humanity lessens
as he kills with glee

Mama Africa weeps for your war
Not for her lullabies sang to you
while she carried your pregnancy
But for the voice of those slavers
Who once held her voice captive

Harken unto the cries
of defenseless men and women
Children languishing
in refugee camps with the remains
of their stolen childhood

La Guerre a gagné

Baldine Moussa

Le mal surgit ! Du sud au nord de l'est à l'ouest,
La terreur fait rage, des larmes se versent,
Ça ne manque pas les cravates et les vestes,
Mais assez de simulacres ! On veut que ça cesse !
Puisque tout le monde nie l'effet, qu'ainsi ça reste !
Les coupables accusent les victimes ! Quelle peste !
Est-ce cette nation qui vend les siens en espèces ?
Les gens se plaignent trop de ces « tristesses ! »
Avec l'oeil de business, et une noire finesse,
Est né l'indifférence, la cruauté et la sècheresse
Des coeurs. Du sang de nos morts, ils s'en nourrissent.
L'argent leur « délivre du mal de la pitié, de la tendresse. »
La compassion et l'amour handicapent le business.
On ne fait pas du profit avec des pleurs et caresses.
On se plaint des morts et du sang qui se verse.
C'est juste quelques milliers d'âmes qui disparaissent
Dans leurs comptes, ce sont des âmes qui se versent,
Ça arrange quelque part ! Le marché progresse !
La dignité humaine voudrait à ce qu'on les laisse
Mourir, les écrabouiller comme des déchets, des restes.
Quelque part on les aide à éviter l'éternelle souffrance,
Qu'ils meurent alors ! Qu'ils le fassent avec délicatesse !
Qu'on les brule, qu'on les enfonce dans les ténèbres terrestres !
Qu'on les aide même à disparaître en silence !
Longtemps, on ne connait que des événements funestes
Chez nous, les sans couleurs ont fait leur partie de chasse.
Manque de satisfaction, ils montent nos âmes traitresses
Les unes contre les autres afin qu'elles se détestent.
La guerre a gagné, on a quitté les terres de nos ancêtres.
On se réfugie loin de chez nous, attend l'aide céleste.
Le pays se vide, les charognards s'en réjouissent.
Videz « pauvres leaders », ce pays de leur substance.
Punaise ! La guerre a gagné, la paix est en vacance.
Je prie, traitres, à ce que l'amour de ce pays vous haïsse !

Ngarbuh Massacre

Prince Wogu Richardson Eyong

Oh, messenger!
Beat the wailing drum,
And summon our ancestors.
Why are they impotent
In the face of such tragedy?
We weep,
They sleep!

Behold the harvest,
Not of corn fields,
Nor of ripe avocados,
But the very souls of civilians,
Burned beyond recognition by the Villains
This is the wedlock of our fate,
Orchestrated from the bedrock of hate!
We cry the foul play,
They hail the fair play!

My heart bleeds,
And breathes sadness
As I tell this story of carnage,
With little or no media coverage.
The world claims life is sacred,
And treasures peace like gold
Yet children and old men alike perish in a massacre.
Is the United Nations nothing but an asshole?
We leave our shells daily in bloodbaths,
And they refresh their souls in warm baths!

We have witnessed our own Holocaust
Tell me, where we have gone wrong!
Is it because we fight a noble cause
That has brought untold misery for so long?
We lament in pains,
They count their gains!

These are the Invaders
Parading our land like the Crusaders,
To unleash the Monarch's wrath,
Oh, there's an appointed day for every rat
Lord, have mercy
And end this adversity!

—16 February 2020

Abakwa

Franklin Agogho

There was that time when mama
In her age-torn wrapper
Whipped me to the stall
To borrow Maggi for soup which was small
After a day in blissful dust
Kicking avocado seeds till
Ngoh bled on nail rust & wailed on lashes,
Served on cane from the mango tree where we stole until it was done

There was that time when I
Held hands with big brother on the road to that house
Where strange children gathered before the talking box
To see white men kiss white girls on crowded streets
And watch Chuck Norris burn fleets like they slept under his feet
Till wisdom stung like a wasp
Dancing on the pang of mama's slap

There was that time
When markets were full of louder shouts
Bigger yams and smaller bags
When customer was family, as money changed hands
And pickpockets picked pockets and not cut bags
When spared purses were chosen by face and not weight
And a 'dash' was law, not the will of some good dame

There was that time
When youth chose dark spots in shady bars
To impress dates who will leave before they knew bad
There was that time when "Mbu bars" courted prestige
Accentuated by bottle dance and wired guitars which graced its bliss
As fathers spewed master political lectures over mugs of palm wine
Choking on laughter, like a strong challenge to beer and its providers

There was that time
When Abakwa was pidgin And pidgin was lingua franca
On neat campuses with students in white socks
But high tongue
In the streets full of yellow taxis
And palace halls, priding in toghus and hailed by cupped claps
"Mbeeeeh"

There was a time when…

And this time? Eh?

Bullets, bangs, blood
Hatred, wretched, fake lords
Father, Spirit, Jesus Christ
Murder, Madness, lost lives
There was when there was Abakwa
Now, ghosts walk the town of laughter

Maybe Rudolf

Ngwa Akongoh

Maybe when the wind of war whooshes
Away
And we sneak out of bushes like rodents —
Darting into our homes—
We will total them up: those many broken helmets,
And ruined swords,
And rusted guns buried in the sand.

Maybe when the sounds of scuffles and
Frightening fracases finally
Die this year,
Famished women
With suckling babes will wobble home
From horrid hideouts to behold brothers' bones broken or
Putrid carcasses swelling in gutters & river banks.

Maybe when the rains of doom stop beating us
And we stroll into the fields again
Where—
Once—
The green grass grew new flower petals,
Our tearful eyes will behold our yawning cadavers
Opened by vultures and witness thoughtless worms
Wriggling in thickest gore.

Maybe their smile and chortles we'll see no more.
Maybe when the wind of war whooshes
Away,
Our onion eyes will look back and sadly behold
Fine footprints of folly on the road we should have left
Untrodden—
Maybe their giggle and laughter we'll see no more.

Maybe.

Crème de Cendre

Josiane Nguimfack

La fumée du désespoir anime les coeurs dès le réveil
Le chant d'oiseaux devient plus funeste jour après jour
Les grillons sortis de leur trou se font piétinés par des sabots
Des sabots durs et pleins de rancunes qui s'acharnent
Semant au passage panique, crainte et désarroi
L'atmosphère poussiéreuse entache les coeurs meurtris
Le chant du coq est remplacé par de cribles de balles matinales
Une douce mélodie qui effraye et avage les âmes déjà en peine
Des villes et des villages sans vie
Des quartiers abandonnés
Les routes volent en éclat et laissent place à des tombeaux ouverts
La douceur d'autrefois écorche la peau avec rage
Des regards vides sans espoir d'un avenir meilleur
Se baladent nonchalamment sur des pistes creuses du désespoir
La peau rocailleuse preuve des longues nuits incertaines
Passées sous la terre au côté des taupes
Qui se voient impuissamment pillé leur domicile
Les écoles sont détruites pour ériger des camps militaires
La règle du jeu est simple, c'est à celui qui tuera plus
Il faut les saigner comme des porcs, c'est tout
Dans cette cacophonie symphonique des balles,
Il n'y a jamais vraiment d'innocents
Jamais de balles perdues, si tu l'as en pleine tête
Tu l'as sûrement mérité et puis c'est tout

What a Weakness
(A Tear for Africa)

Ekpe Inyang

What a weakness fighting
with a crippled person
using your strong muscles
on a muscles-less being
what a shame

What a shame
facing a blind person
in a boxing or wrestling ring
using all your tactics
what a weakness

What a weakness
declaring war on the unarmed
ready with battalions, armored
vehicles, helicopters and all
what a shame

What a shame
invading defenseless villages
using your military might,
weapons and ammunitions
what a weakness

What a weakness
deliberately shooting at people
with hands up, begging
children crawling on the floor
what a shame

What a shame
burning down houses
of poor villagers after you
frightened them into bushes
what a weakness

What a weakness
facing the lanky brother
of the muscular one
who just beat you in a fight
what a shame

—19 January 2020

Ceremony of the Unattended

Nnane Ntube

Did you know my people have a ceremony?
Fancy driven?
Twists of tongues gave birth to words that danced in the vacuum of our streets,
Words that fell on placid soil like a thunderbolt.
Obese legs nuzzled the soil
And squelched bloody potholes.
We squatted,
On lines they told us not to toe,
Left to gather dust and cobwebs,
And this, they called our ceremony?
Oh, let my thoughts visit the unconscious
And dialogue with the conscious!
Let me say "yes" to this or "no"!
If you had been a prisoner,
You would've understood the suffocating need
For me to dance the song my people sing.
That hand that squeezed my voice in its bag of political madness
Has ended up begetting monsters.

L'Obscurité du jour

Z-Ulrich de Dieu

Le ciel n'est plus clair comme à l'accoutumée
Pour côtoyer la beauté de ses étoiles
Tragédies et guerres deviennent ses citoyens
Un soleil triste s'est lassé devant la nudité du temps
Il pousse sur la couleur du drapeau camerounais
Un espoir scié par les violeurs des droits
Que dire des mauvais vents qui le déstabilisent ?
Cameroun danse au rythme de toutes tragédies de l'Afrique
Les pleurs des uns font la grande joie des autres
Et les larmes des uns arrosent le jardin des autres
Je hurle et crie jusqu'à déchirer ma gorge
Quand je vois sa dignité avortée
Par le sourire hypocrisié des institutions
La paix et la guerre liées au vent
Se disputent pour son destin masqué
Destin égorgé par la barbarie humaine
Le sang de milliers de ses fils et filles
Jonche sa terre d'ébène à perpétuité
Un puit de pétrole en vaux la vie de l'être
Pour faire fonctionner la machine de bonheur
De ses va-nu-pieds venus de mille continents
La cendre de ma mémoire s'est éreintée
Devant l'obscurité du jour, voir le visage
De chaque natif camerounais
Inondé par un fleuve de malheur
Les cris incendient les oreilles calfatées par les obus
L'absence prolongée du sommeil invite les noeuds de ténèbres
Pour séquestrer l'instant présent de la vie
Cameroun n'a plus des femmes et d'églises
Cameroun n'a plus des hommes et des greniers
Cameroun n'a plus des rêves et d'avenir
Tout subsiste au prix de la cendre de pénitence
La paix est blessée tel le nuage par le vent sceptique
Dans cette tragédie il faut réinventer la vie
Pour s'échapper au poids de la mort
Au coup des assassinats causés par les christs
Et semeurs de misère, armés jusqu'aux dents
La philanthropie s'est lassée devant les actes insensés
De l'homme du siècle qui poignarde l'éducation, la dignité
La paix, par le crépitement de l'âme d'Autrui
Pour ne psalmodier que des drames assaisonnés
Afin de se réjouir de l'effacement brutal du Cameroun

Sur la carte Africaine sacrifiée depuis lustres temps
Sur l'autel de l'argent par les hommes d'ailleurs
Je nous appelle à la paix ô natifs camerounais !
Faisons de la réconciliation notre reine
Le dialogue notre roi pour ne plus voir
La vie de chaque natif, baobab, enseignant,
S'écroulée comme les veines de la bougie
Je ne dors pas en paix, quand j'entends
Par les pas du vent les pleurs amers du Cameroun
Traversés les frontières de la mort d'un long gémissement
Je ne manifeste non plus l'étincèle de mon sourire
Quand le nombre de ceux qui traversent le royaume des ombres
S'accumule, quelle qu'elle soit l'obscurité du jour
La lumière de la paix finira par scintiller nos coeurs
Afin de repenser l'avenir de notre Afrique.

The Fall of Tyrants

Dr Sadiqullah Khan

They one by one fell
Went to hiding the little tyrants –
Wolves and hungry beasts
They a pack of the crumbling empire
Of the underworld –
They who drank blood
Of the innocent and fed on flesh
Who were hired assassins
They for penny would commit murder
Or name any heinous crime –
They are the ugliest form
Of repression –
They under the garb of law
Under protection brutally kill –
Torture and demean
They rape and thrive on thievery
But they can't stand a truth
Their thirty thousand lies
And your one truth –
They break apart quickly
Lacking in moral cohesion they
Since are characterless
Brutal and cruel
They are hardened and seasoned
Criminals –
They are an enemy of humans
Flourishing in political uncertainty
They are gangsters –
A respectable citizen fears them
Like a nightmare
Living vampires on day light,
Cowards of the first order
They know that they are above law
Above any discipline
They look like dacoits on the lose
They are capable
They are well connected
For they are either dons
Or servants to a Don –
A saleable commodity
Revengeful and vindictive
They are armed with lethal weapons –

They kill with impunity Staging an encounter –
They think that they will get away
With it, – but for how long?

Les Enfants du Président

Samy Manga

Assis sur le plexus d'un drapeau correctement travesti, les enfants du Président dormiront jusqu'au crépuscule de la finitude, affalés comme des porcs empiffrés de trois-mille fongicides, ils regarderont la télévision tout au long des sanglants décrets, en famille et même en cercle vicieux, ils applaudiront la vigueur du parti tout au long de la vie, en ingurgitant la bile courtisane d'un gouvernant sexagénaire.

Comme des castors lettrés en destruction sournoise, ils mangeront les veines et les tendons du corps national, ils boiront son squelette et la chair pâle d'une économie sale avec les pépins de sa justice, sans jamais savoir sur quoi est bâtie la brûlure de la ville éteinte. Ils iront simplement à l'école des lois, puis à la Faculté de droit. Des nouvelles du front, ils n'en sauront jamais rien qui vaille la peine d'être su, de toute façon, il n'y a rien à savoir, de l'autre côté de la République, ils n'y seront pas, ils n'y vivront jamais, ni près du sang saillant des estropiés, ni près des bébés violés, ni près du feu cru prolétarien au sexe écrasé.

Une armée de folles altitudes enterre le meurtre politique, la presse étatique joue son rôle de camoufleur, les charognards sucent la moelle lacérée des corps collatéraux, le firmament tombe, les bombes fleurissent dans le regard des enfants, les uns meurent pour le drapeau et la majorité pour l'ivoire du pétrole. Âgé de quelques années d'innocences, le crâne insurgé est un trou béant, le souffle des canons égorge sa iberté.

Pénitences et croix cruelles au coeur de la patrie, la guerre est une belle manne que seuls les rois savent aduler, un général n'est général que lorsqu'il sait affûter les sorts du carnage, sculptant l'ennemi, lui donnant une nomination, une physionomie, une trajectoire, une date de péremption, puis une terre d'exil bien à ride et sans aucune devise. Pour dire l'autorité, les hommes de pouvoir savent piétiner les petits cadavres qu'ils appellent Peuple, saignant les virginités mineures contre les crosses des chevrotines, ils savent fouler les ossements humains avec une étrange fermeté détachée de toutes sensations.

Dans un pays fait de pères déchirés et de lois fissurées, les mères ne sont plus des femmes à promouvoir devant un tel torrent de barbarie inondant le vestige historique de la Paix calcinée, et celui de la Mémoire civilisationnelle immolée.

Lorsque les armes grondent dans le gosier des éléphants, les rescapés et les petites personnes marchent avec la nuit, marchent avec le jour, marchent avec leurs intestins dans les bras, hurlant dans la gueule d'un ciel terriblement muet, criant dans la poitrine d'une terre complètement anéantie. Pour un brin d'espérance, ils s'effondrent dans le lac des abîmes pendant que d'autres, déshumanisés, courent vers le traquenard des urnes. À travers les monts, les rivières de crevettes, et les hostilités forestières de la Menchum, les désoeuvrés couchent des larmes de peine comme des fresques devant un continent silencieux périssant dans un sommeil trop colonisé.

La guerre est un dîner souverain avec des invités de marque
La guerre est une belle manne que seule la dictature sait aduler. Demain ne sera plus demain Aujourd'hui étant ontologiquement décédé
La vie a cessé d'exister
Avec toi
Avec moi
Avec nous.

Heda Te Bia Ku Suam

Cameroon, the Valley of Death

Mbizo Chirasha

Cameroon,
You cannot drink your own eggs in the name of expediency.
You cannot slash wombs in daylight and
Let your machetes drink blood of children in dawns of violence.
Once beautiful earth watered with tears and sweat;
You're lost in the valley of death!

Cameroon,
You've grown war canines.
What a death-mongering warlord!
Shelling and pounding human flesh like millet!

Cameroon,
Tell me what is anglophone and what is francophone.
Humanity is one.
Why perish children and kill mothers for not speaking your language?
Humans are humans.

Cameroon,
You're everyone's country.
So, we cry Freedom.
We sing of Peace.
We cry Freedom for Anglophone Cameroon.
Let tomorrow's Sun rise with rays of
Peace and the glow of Freedom!

Google Southern Cameroons and Shame on Us, All!

MD Mbutoh

In the secured shell of my house,
Hidden in the 'enemy' camp,
I read The distressing messages of a
Mother over her four-month-old sent
To eternal slumber by soldiery bullets!

It may have the voice of fiction,
Until you google it to see how fiction
Materialises to reality— games of death whence
Soldiers made incisions in
the body of an infant, dear silent world!

"They forced their way into the house...
shot my baby who was sleeping while I was in the kitchen,
no matter how much I begged them...
The military did that...I place a curse on them
for doing this to my child...these tears I shed will never go in vain..."

—The mother of the four-month-old baby
shot in Muyuka today...reported
The tabloids and media, shifting the fear of being the
Next in the arena of death.

This is a fine place, bedevilled with
Bad seeds whose taproots sink into
Innocent bodies to give the system life.
States, they say monopolize violence...even human rights?
Even before the face of innocence?
How long? Google Southwest & Northwest of
Cameroon: it is no movie comrades!

The gun cannot vomit before the pen,
For it is the pen's vomit that commands the trigger,
And the fall of the body follows after.
Huts cannot cackle if keyboards don't
Jump in foreign mouse-holes, for it is sycophancy that mutes young ambition.

Ghosts cannot depart their temples if
Was the finger that killed my neighbour & the infant.
When hens hide their chicks in foreign
Holes and stand amid neighbours' yards
And dare kites to a fight,

Such a kinsman would crush your testicle
For pleasure, and on them shall he build
Kubla Khan's chasm whence demon dark,
Demon lovers roam the hoods and wake
Angry souls to take vengeful steps into
The dance arena...

When the sun closes its lips and the moon
Hides from the evil of man, even the mud
Bricks of Peuchop Ndop, are no longer safe...
Yesterday a kin fell among thieves from
A sibling's bullet, before the dreadful
Eyes of his two or three infants...

Who will hold these young bullets when
They go loose, searching for their father's killers?
A good son always kills the killer of his father.
A common hate, the poet said, enraged
Us all, and a callous act took from us
The ancient memories of pride and zeal!

When daggers are pillows and spears
Are anvils on which dark buttocks heat,
Surely broken bottles shall be the path on
Which all of us shall walk.
Interred within are angels and demons,
But stronger is the will to decide...no?

Shame on us, all! Shame on us, All!
No!

Shame on those leaving the stage earlier,
For their brothers who send them off
So valiantly professed kinship to the tyrants!
Shame on us at oedipal sunrise!
Shame on us at Hamlet noon!
Shame on us at octogenarian ev'ning dinner!

La Jungle nous a surpris

Beaton Galafa

La mort vient dans toutes les tailles
Pour nous c'est tellement cruelle
Elle est venue dans les bottes et les armes à feu
Et les garçons et les hommes et les machettes
J'avais menti à mes enfants qu'après
que le soleil s'est levé nous nous sommes égarés
de la solitude que le monde offre
Ils nous ont incarcérés quand ils ont
pensé que nous étions tout autre animal qu'ils
Pourraient mettre en cage et pour cela je suis désolé.

Je dois présenter des excuses
À mes filles et leurs mères
parce que je ne les ai pas préparés à quoi
la jungle avait en réserve.
Si je leur avais dit que ce serait le même cycle
de leurs âmes lavées dans le sang qui coule à la mer
Si je leur avais dit que leurs héros se régaleraient
avec les renards et boivent leur sang
et écrasent leurs os
à la table d'honneur pendant que leurs cris résonnaient
dans les longs couloirs étroits du pouvoir qui s'étendaient
à des kilomètres au-delà de leurs frontières
Peut-être auraient-ils attendu calmement la mort chez eux—
avec leurs coeurs ne battant pas dans les forêts comme ils l'ont fait
quand le gouvernement et les séparatistes voulaient tous les sacrifier
aux dieux de la guerre.

Cameroon Rouge

Goodenough Mashego

some games don't have names
so, we call them the crying game
when the director yells 'cut' the orgy ceases
paramedics invade the pitch
wolves lick their mane as they disappear in a ditch
hospital casualty wards line their porters
mortuaries sanitize their slabs
pathologists slide on fresh surgical gloves
Blood Bank begs for group O negative
today they test not for HIV nor hepatitis B

some people partake in games that have no names
they wear armour carry machetes they are stars of our shame
battle themselves hoping to survive self-emulation
out of one should prevail a winner & loser when the sun sets
we cut our noses to spite our faces
like van gogh slice off my left ear so i hear not my tongue sing
God Bless the Queen give her another jubilee
La Marseillaise forget not the 1789 revolution
why play a game with goal posts in France and Britain
when mother Africa is music i sing her a lullaby
-ends-

Cécité

Ray Ndebi

Pourquoi faut-il que j'aie à présent peur
Moi qui pouvais traverser mon village
Le vivre par ses vallées et ses hauteurs
J'étais à la maison à chaque rivage

Chaque main tendue était la main d'un frère
Et chaque sourire était celui d'une soeur
Nous avions le Cameroun comme même mère
Nos langues s'épanouissaient dans un seul choeur

Pour quelle raison donc, qu'on vienne me le dire
Mon sourire doit avoir l'éclat d'une lame
Et mon pays qui sous une étoile peut luire
Ira par plusieurs morceaux perdre son âme

Des bannières dressent déjà leur arrogance
Défiant tous les cieux de la Liberté
Clamant par le sang leur indépendance
Et le feu brûle l'espoir de l'Unité

Est-ce seulement cela qu'on a voulu
Quand on a brandi la démocratie
Comme le soleil qui rassemble dans les rues
Nous voici rampant vers l'ambazonie

Qu'appelle-t-on Cameroun anglophone
Quelle est cette terre qui me paraît une île
J'entends parler de ce peuple ambazone
Comme d'une race à l'esprit très peu fertile

J'entends dire que ces âmes du good morning
Ne connaissent pas le même matin que moi
Leur réveil, semble-t-il, est juste nothing
Si elles ne s'accommodent pas à ma voie

J'entends dire que là-bas tout est travers
Et qu'on doit se lever comme le colon
Pour les soumettre par le feu ou le fer
Comme nous tous durant les siècles du coton

Ô qu'il est loin le temps où nous étions
Un seul coeur dans un seul corps… qu'il est loin
Ce temps où s'entendait rugir le lion
Qu'il est loin ce temps, pourtant là au coin

Qu'avons-nous fait de notre grande mémoire
L'héritage de notre mère est-il perdu
S'il est vrai que nous n'avons pas d'histoire
Pour quel futur nous sommes-nous donc battus

Peut-on effacer de ce vif présent
Les familles que nous bâtissons sans cesse
Nous avons le sourire de nos enfants
A préserver de cette aveugle détresse

N'avons-nous pas compris que l'aube nouvelle
Ce paradis enseigné aux pupilles
Ne sert pas juste à meubler la cervelle
D'un jour valide qui contemple ses béquilles

Huit provinces ne font pas de moi un maître
Deux provinces ne t'obligent pas en victime
Aux yeux de notre mère, nous sommes tous deux traitres
Vu combien la haine nous devient intime

Où est mon village, le sein de ma chair
Les entrailles qui ont forgé ma fierté
Il n'y aura que des ruines sous le calvaire
Et des larmes pour le pays tout entier

A chaque goutte de larme versée par une mère
Une fille, une veuve, une soeur ou une amie
La douleur ne sera pas étrangère
Elle n'aura pas de langue, elle sera d'ici

Elle ne restera pas à Bamenda
Son tambour roulera à Yaoundé
Son tamtam battra très fort à Douala
Oui, loin aussi de Buéa et Limbé

La *crise anglophone* n'est que cette fumée
Dont le feu est vif sous tout le triangle
Chers saigneurs, je n'ai pas peur de saigner
Je mourrai mille morts pour le vivre-ensemble

Puisque vous l'avez décidé ainsi
Aveugles et égoïstes, vous ignorez
Tous autant que vous êtes, tous, bien assis
Qu'elle est déjà ici, la Liberté…

2017-2019 Earthquake

Kile Rash Ike

Two brothers, twin-cultures divided by river; just a river.
Brother grieved at brother; his home is yard margin.
His culture and belief values are facing swallow.
He wants fair take of the family props.
These agonies pierce into his soul as barbed wires.
His life gallows and gallops as flat tyres.

His brother across river plays decades deaf and dumb mouth.
Now, accuses brother of bogus and sham.
So, their love and peace froze to stone.
Love and unity stood dead and hate as tough as bone.

Oh! They debate with iron and steel.
None to quench the brawl but UN, yet father
UN watches as palapala tournament!
Death oust souls and slashing limbs gain scene.
Anger and terror reign as diseases and escape gain fame.
UN silent as bribed policeman,
In snail speed sighed at it and spoke grammar
Which could not cold brothers' red-boiling magma.
Oh! UN is but a grammar teacher, not a discipline master!
The World is yet to taste destruction!

The Quake of an Innocent Corpse

Franklin Agogho

It feels like the gong heralds its own news
Because the town crier ran to the bush.

It feels like the birds lost their wings
And now crawl the earth, scratching like hens on heat.

If feels like tomorrow feared its way
And choose to come yesterday.

If feels like goodness is strapped to a post
And raped by dogs who reign like fools at the crossroads.

It feels like a dream
That Prudence embraced grinning death
Surfing on a bullet whose initiator lurks in the shadows
Because she wears the uniform
Of police,
Though her kind still wobble at the academy.

From cubicles stacked with artificial air,
Their screams went to the base,
"Send them out, there is no better practice for their case,"
Though, in stolen suits, they forgot
That dead men, in wars, do not fear a situation lesser than their case.

Yes. Dead men!
Dead by the pangs of pain from lashes on their ego.
Dead for lack of home settled in the arms of another's control.
Dead from hunger grown so normal, it has become a chore.
Dead for need of escape, so much that denial invited madness to the floor.

But Prudence took the bullet.
The rookie, in a starless uniform, who still learned the run,
Clasped the rifle with sweaty hands,
And took the bullet. Her brains spilling like a painting on a theatre stage.

It feels like I see headless men in choirs rehearsing the peace song.

It feels like I need a wand and black magic,
To blow to normalcy my soul and my shattered wits.

Mon Afrique

Gbeada Maxence

Mon Afrique se meurt d'une mort moribonde
Tant d'atrocités commises pour des intérêts égocentriques
Oui le Cameroun se ridiculise, se divise et se meurt
Les flammes de la haine, les réverbères d'obscurité ont assombri ce beau pays
Le cri sans voix et calciné des éventrés, des égorgés, des violées monte dans
 l'atmosphère
Un bain de sang envahissant toute les ruelles comme l'inondation de Sodome et
 Gomorrhe
ONU, UA, impuissantes face à ces dérives aux conséquences barbares
La barbarie est montée au créneau, les dirigeants égoïstes, les présidents avides et
 fiers de leur moi
Ne privilégiant pas l'intérêt du peuple mais ceux de leurs vaines gloires passagères
Mon Afrique se meurt d'une mort moribonde
Mon Afrique où rime vers, danse, musique et bonheur
Mon Afrique de l'or, de diamant et bien d'autres ressources s'asphyxie
Mon Afrique à besoin d'une prise de conscience messianique de tous ses enfants
Mon Afrique a besoin de la solidarité, mon Afrique à besoin de l'Amour
Oui d'un Amour fraternel, et non d'un amour de l'égo où rime hypocrisie et
 vengeance
Sauvons l'Afrique, Sauvons le Cameroun
Oui Sauvons l'Afrique.

Things Fall Apart

Star Okpeh

Vain songs
Vain lies
Blood cries in our minds
Where war is now a maddened cross
Chewing the future apart.

We stand idle
Wondering
Dark. Still and bloody
The village sits in mourning.

Mothers dream of something
Lost from our wrists
Where is the bracelet of our peace?

A child runs out with broken bones
Dripping out of him.
Of all there is, nothing is left
If violence takes the lead.

la rue est une femme

Géraldin Mpesse

la rue est une femme
affectueuse qui accueille
des rescapés du massacre
qui déambulent sur les pas feutrés du désespoir

la rue est l'écueil qui recèle
la souffrance des hommes dont le feu
des canons a léché les demeures

la rue est l'abattoir humain où ruissèle
le sang des frères qui s'entretuent froidement
pour complaire la main invisible

la rue est le pupitre où les frères du NOSO
chantent leurs misères pour que naisse
un jour nouveau

The Politics of Deafness

Nancy Ndeke

O Cameroon,
Haven't you seen the bloodied brothers?
In Rwanda,
In South Sudan,
And learnt the outcomes,
That talking keeps at bay bloodletting?
O land of our sane brothers,
For long living with hope,
Dividing by communication that should thaw differences.
But now,
Simmering murmurs
And banners screams,
Men in suits and naked dead litter your streets.
O Cameroon,
Language binds,
Not divides.
Language builds,
Not destroys.
Have you not seen the piled up skulls
Of children and elders before their time?
Have you not seen
Boat-loads of fleeing souls
Turning up belly-up on foreign shores?
O Cameroon, touch your cheeks and wake up,
Before history writes your story
In bloodied ink as so many on this continent
Have done for the deafness of their leaders.

On ne compte pas les cadavres noirs

Nsah Mala

Soyez les bienvenus au Cameroun
Où une sale guerre a enterré l'unité
Pour ressusciter une union sacrée !
Mais non, j'allais dire une union sanglante.

Dans des fosses communes en brousse
Sont entassées des semences humaines
De l'unité et
De la division.

Or, les fusils ne peuvent pas façonner
Le vivre-ensemble,
Car celui-ci se négocie au quotidien
Comme un couple négocie son amour.

D'ailleurs,
L'omniprésence des guerres et des conflits
Démasquent l'incapacité des groupes budgétivores
Comme l'Onu et l'Union africaine.

N'est-ce pas l'Elysée est sourd-muet ?
Allez-vous-en avec vos chiffres de morts.
A l'Elysée, on mesure les barils du pétrole ;
Pas du temps pour compter les cadavres noirs.

Tant que Paris ne hausse pas le ton,
Tant que Paris ne sort pas un carton rouge,
Ses petits gouverneurs de l'outre-mer
Boivent du sang noir à la santé de la coopération !

Il faut toujours se rappeler
Qu'un tas de cadavres nègres ne vaut pas la peine.
C'est la joie pour certains activistes écologiques !
C'est plus d'accès aux ressources souterraines !

Yaoundé peut donc uriner des bombes partout
Chers les anglos, car on ne compte pas les cadavres noirs.

—*Aarhus, le 17 septembre 2019*

Lines and Tongues
[for Cameroon]

Goodenough Mashego

the pinky drew a line in the sand
& called it a boundary
so red ants from the north
shall not cross to the south
those that call the north home
shall know not about the south

about that life of plenty
that they live in the north
share not in trials & tribulations
they suffer in the south
north meets not south
only through shadows when
the sun sets & rises shall they hug

pinky drew another line on my tongue
called it a linguistic barrier
so francophone meets not anglo
neither anglo does francophone
merci shall mean not thank you
nor thank you mean merci
for we tasted the cyanide with the tip of our tongues

Ma Maison

Josiane Nguimfack

C'est où ma maison
Question existentielle
Réponse existentielle

C'est où ma maison
Est-ce là où crèvent des enfants
S'installe l'analphabétisme
Naissent les enfants l'arme à la main

C'est où ma maison
Est-ce là où le sang coule comme de l'eau
La vue des corps dépecés est naturelle
Décapiter c'est le quotidien

C'est où ma maison
Est-ce là où la faim et le viol cohabitent
La déportation à feu grégeois règne
Les morts enterrent les morts

C'est où ma maison
Est-ce là où la liberté est lancée à bâbord
Le dialogue a pris la clé d'escampette
Rester coi est la règle d'or

C'est où ma maison
Est-ce là où mes investissements s'évaporent
Dans l'air âcre des troubles et de la révolte
Se fait tuer au passage n'est que malchance

C'est où ma maison
C'est où
C'est alors où hein
Merde elle est où ma chienne de maison

Majority and Minority

Nancy Ndeke

Is man not man,
Whether the bigger house or the small one?
Is man not flesh and blood,
If he speaks Europe or Eurasia?
Is man not a creation's creature?
Whether assimilated or adopted,
A crisis looms,
One more time,
Over century issues that under the carpet got swept,
And the ugly step child bastard of secession,
Rumbles in the valleys and hills of a people sharing food and lovers.
What happens when inclusivity and dialogue are bastardized?
What happens when free and fair appointments
Are lassoed like cow boy gams?
Violence springs like overnight mushrooms,
And rivers of anger burst banks to smoother speech,
And old grudges surface,
To cry old wounds.
Even as we write poetry,
A land awaits grave-diggings,
Unknown yet known,
A curse doing experiments everywhere in Africa.
The sorry story of seeds of discord long planted,
And we're the harvesters of tidal tears,
Because power renders us drunk
And greed dances on state houses
Where common sense has been replaced by ignorance.

Cameroun !

Luc Koffi

Combien de fois le sang innocent
Versera sur ces routes pourpres du Cameroun ?
Combien de soldats, de civils sont sortis et ne sont plus revenus ?
Combien d'hôpitaux incendiés, de villages calcinés, de réfugiés volatilisés ?
Ô Cameroun ! Regarde tes enfants qui passent qui courent qui tombent,
Sous le bruit sourd des tanks.
Demain, ils grandiront surement dans des pays voisins.
Regarde tes filles tes femmes qui se lamentent pour se sauver du tourment.
Demain, elles t'arracheront certainement ta pérennité.
Regarde le temps qui court sous nos yeux,
Et nous laisse : ruines, famine et misères.
Sauve tes enfants, sauve l'éducation !
Sauve tes femmes, sauve l'avenir !
Sauve-toi, sauve la paix !
Car demain, le temps passera par là
Et nous laissera de fétides souvenirs :
Souvenirs de morts, tristes souvenirs d'un Cameroun déchiré.
Ô Cameroun ! Sauve-toi et réconcilie-toi pour l'avenir de tes enfants.

It's Midnight in Yaoundé

Michael Mwangi Macharia

When the world wakes
From eternal unbroken reverie
To reality of a country
Torn apart by foreign tongues;

When the mass graves
Tucked with innocent villagers
Those that couldn't ballot
Celebrated with hail of bullets;

When the grim reality
Of hapless shepherds in collars
Armed with crucifixes and oil
Swept by the raging storm;

When a continent is roused
From slumber of inaction
Too shamed to look at itself
At the mirror another time;

Will there be a country left
To rebuild from dust and ashes?

Her Silence

Nsah Mala

Suddenly she went mute
Like an unmoving stone.
Her silence throbbed
Across voids.
Asked why, she muttered:

The tree in their yard
Was shaking violently
As angry gusts of wind
Slapped it, blaming it
For identities sliding
Down throats of mambas.
Oracles from far and near
Diagnosed its rotting roots:

They urged elders to unearth
The tree, balm its sick roots
And replant; but they chose
To prune branches, to caress leaves,
As its decaying roots creaked
Underneath, its trunk tilting
In ferocious sways.
And she borrowed muteness
From the wise Tortoise
To seek shelter before its fall.

—*Santiago de Compostela, 08 March 2018*

Ballot or Barrel

Reagan Ronald Ojok

The spirit of your ancestors is calling—
Wake up from your political anesthesia
Wake up from the bondage of sniffing in overdose the political fart
Ballot or barrel, rise up in unity to claim your freedom

Ubuntu Yaoundé .... Ubuntu Cameroon!
Our comrades_
The power of a united people
Is stronger than the people in power
Rise up Cameroon, rise above the water,
To liberate your future from political captivity

We worship a loving God
He shall not abandon us in the hands of dictatorship
When oppression crowds out basic rights—
Then tyranny begins to germinate!
Fear not thy fangs of oppression
For African Union is sleeping
It is too drunk with power
To save your nation

La Parodie

Baldine Moussa

Coeurs malades, coeurs trompés, de nous, de vous,
Ames courtisées, volées, violées puis abandonnées
Mères de nous, de vous endeuillées et abusées !
Êtres privés de liberté de joie, de paix par les autres ;
Riches de terres, de ressources, mais pauvres d'amour
Outrepassés par la ruse de nos grands ennemis
Utilisés pour tuer et maltraiter nos frères de germe
N'avons-nous pas encore compris leur ruse ?
A quel moment penserons à ce mal mettre un terme?
Interrogeons-nous de cette vie, mensonge éternel,
Sentez en, je vous en prie cet arrière-goût de sang
On vous sert à la place de la bière du sang
Ne voyez-vous pas ? La chanson manque de rythme ?
Vous-même, prêtez oreille, c'est de la pire parodie.
Orner une salle ne fait pas en soit la réussite d'une fête
Usons de nos sens, sortons de notre sommeil !
Sortons de notre rêve éternel, c'est un cauchemar
Trouver refuge auprès des autres ne suffit pas
Rester passifs fera de nous des complices
Osons vomir les faux cadeaux qu'on nous sert.
« Merde ! » Disons-le, afin de nous libérer du joug !
Parler, qu'on soit camerounais ou cameroonian,
English ou French, ne dois pas nous diviser…

Martha

Prince Wogu Richardson Eyong

I hear mourning drums
echo in distant lands.
Martha has withered like a flower
in the absence of her mother
to the world of no return.
What crime for this four-month old infant?
Shall fortunes redeem her hasty sleep?
Oh, the wonder of human barbarism!
I see dark clouds
loom around Muyuka.
Martha's hasty departure
paints the picture of such atrocities
meted out by deadly scorpions.
What crime for this four-month-old baby?
This is the monstrous cowardice of war mongers!
Mother of Martha,
wail no more.
I smell the verdict of Heaven
oozing like a volcano
to render justice for Martha's gruesome death.
Oh, what crime for this four-month-old baby?

Victims

Tatah Allen Laika

Boom! boom! boom! boom!
Pim! pim! pim! pim! pim!
The thunderous echoes of the landlord.
AK 47? Dane gun? grenades? bomb?
The sound confuses us.
Who will tell us?
No one can even if he wants to.
Streets deserted; houses orphaned.
We run, we fly, we limp, we slide.
Going home, safe home.
In the bush we always find solace.
A God-given refugee camp.
At times we spend the night.
Yet we are comfortable.
Animals were enjoying that we never knew.
Animals so hospitable,
They leave as we arrive.
Animals safeguard our departed ones.
They touch not the anointed.
Yet we spare not the anointed.
We call them animals and they see us as "Manimals."
The "Go home" sound sends them "home" too.
Bullets fly above us like Russian roulettes.

They are cheerful and indiscriminate givers.
Givers of pain, chagrin, pathos and doom.
Poor things, they know not who to spare.
Children they shatter, elders they batter, youths they scatter.
Who is safe? Houses? Churches? Shops?
No! No! No! None is free, all are guilty.
Inferno grips an innocent building,
Burglary woos a commercial centre.

Oh humanity! Oh sanity! Oh humility!
Why were you so cheap? Pure cowards.
Why did you turn your back on us?
Inhumanity, insanity, insolence: dreaded foes,
Strange bed fellows.
You give me nightmares.
No, you give me insomnia.
Why are you so intolerant?
Why are you so cruel?

You forget so soon!
But I must remind you
That you shall not kill.
Thou can't create breath.

Cowards, feeble minds, hypocrites.
You wrestle not with your matches,
You attack your own, yet you say you protect them.
Elephants trample on the grass.
Ooh the once greenish grass,
Now a desert you have become!

Caught in a chaotic web.
People say you must survive.
Yes, they say so but what next?
You are orphans, vomited by mother earth.
You are the sacrificial lambs.
You are playthings of the wanton boys.
For how long shall you be a bait?
When you smile they say you are laughing at them.
Cry and you are patronizing the fiends.
Orphans, victims, cowards, preys! You are.
Protégés, civilians, humans they call you.
Animals, flies, statues you actually are.

You are not happy.
You are sad.
You are not lucky.
You are doomed.
You aren't silent.
You are vocal.
They are instead deaf.
The noise of your troubled heart is vivid.
The cacophony of your traumatic mind is ignored.
Your silence is conspicuous.
It speaks volumes.
God, give them an attentive ear,
To listen to the wails of Adam's descendants,
To restore to them that which they lack more:
Peace, peace, peace.
God, pee your drops of peace on us.
Let's talk.

Disent les victimes dans leur silence

Nsah Mala

Nous sommes les fameuses herbes
Qui souffrent quand deux éléphants se bagarrent,
Disent les victimes dans leur silence.

Les Amba Boys nous enferment
Dans nos propres maisons les jours des lockdowns.
Personne ne sort, même pour aller au champs
Chercher quoi manger ; on n'a que faim du changement.
Personne ne sort, même pour aller à l'hôpital,
Car pendant la guerre les maladies apprennent
A nous donner des rendez-vous avant de venir.
Un enfant qui veut sortir du ventre
Ne doit jamais choisir un jour de lockdown
Parce que the struggle must continue !

Arrivent alors nos vaillants Soldats
Qui, remplis du professionnalisme, brûlent nos maisons
A la recherche des Amba Boys
Ou pour nous punir de les soutenir
Ou simplement pour déverser leurs colères après des pertes.
Nos semences, nos aliments, nos animaux, nos documents
Disparaissent tous en cendres et en fumées de l'unité.
Les spirales de ces fumées annoncent le pape de l'église chaotique
Qui nous attend dans notre diversité, dans notre vivre-ensemble.
Les fumées des hôpitaux vont bander nos plaies de division,
Car traiter un séparatiste blessé est un crime contre l'unité !

Nous sommes les fameuses herbes
Qui souffrent quand deux éléphants se bagarrent,
Disent les victimes dans leur silence.

—Aarhus, le 17 septembre 2019

Miracles

Omadang Yowasi

Don't tell me of the stench,
It's chocking my nostrils.
What did they do
To deserve what you offer?
Children dwelling in the wild
With children of the cobra.
How do you love a brother
By chasing him with a sword?
Bamenda is mourning,
Yaoundé is smiling,
Bafoussam is flourishing,
But they're just watching.
Hope's hidden far beyond.
With the deafening silence,

And a day that passes by
Is what we count as a miracle.

Brother's Plea

Kile Rash Ike

Brother, brother, think.
Think brother, think of yesterday.
Yesterday of milk and honey,
Of love launching a thousand smile.
Peace was the displaying profile
And unity shielding pending danger.
From ripening dawn to fading twilight
In happy streets of busy passers-by
Life was a calm cool lullaby.
Did you not love it?

But hey! Brother HEEY!
Brother, brother, see?
See today is drowning in a sea
Of weary dreary quarrels
Of ghosting streets dropping souls
In the chorusing booming riffles.
Dying humanity weeps and baffles
This Clinging creepy cringing piercing agony
Rising from the yellow sun to the red sun.

Taar! Taar! TAAR! TAAR!
Is what choruses
Our air now, stinking with stench of blood.
On our streets crimson flows.
Black tarmac painted with gut slime.
Ululations of men…ululations of men?
Screams of men, screams of scared men!
Never have I seen grown-ups cry
Nor saw them run from homestead to monkeys' jungle!

Taar! Taar! TAAR! TAAR!
Have born corpses here and there
In pools of crimson red
Infested my mother with onion eyes
Threatening our breathe at all alleys.
She seeks refuge in monkeys' jungle
With heavy child on her back.
Mother and crying hungry child
Make a feast for mosquitoes
In the dark torrential mists.

A grey-haired grandmother labours over a pickaxe
And the desert sun baking her withered skin.
The Harmattan's pity for her releases pensive sighs.
She tries to create decent graves

For her husband, her son and her grandson!
Mourning no longer fashionable.
How many shall you mourn?
Oh humanity is bereaved, bereaved, bereaved!
When shall we be relieved?

Walk upon our soil of bereaved faces,
Soil of stench, of gushing feces from torn-out guts.
Land where, mothers smile
As they see their sons fall,
Happy that they have a day yet to live.
Are souls thirsty for love in fears
And begging for peace in tears?
For the shield of humanity is unity.

Oh Brother! Brother ooh!
Drop down your booming riffle
To make mankind baffle.
Sons of the same womb do not dagger.

buvons, mon frère

Géraldin Mpesse

mon frère,
trinquons à la santé
des discoureurs qui attisent
le feu de l'adversité
et nous chantent les valeurs
d'une mère qu'ils ont étranglée

buvons, mon frère
buvons
pour célébrer la quatrième année
de la fructueuse récolte du sang
et sous nos pas de danse frénétiques
écrasons les germes d'espoir qui affleurent

Golden Star from the Mud

Wisdom Zachariah

Oh…cradle of your forebears
Cameroon…Ruined?
Pre-1960, bled for your liberation, but you still bleed!
Martyrs of the south
Taught you the scout…To kill thousands
But you killed tens of thousands.
Uncooked blood! … How it tastes!
Only the weapons of homeless Avenger…know!
Poor Avengers…Heeding politicians is that all you know?
The parables of war!
Female genitals undressed, rape! … death!
Children dragged from breast into the blades
Nurses treated in wounds
Teachers sampled for murder
Blood! Burnings! Bloody! … Wars!
Dead bodies, like refuse decorating the streets
Plants fearing germination … To hell!
Even animals share the hate

Les Anges de la mort

Beaton Galafa

J'étais là quand ils sont venus
Je m'étais accroché aux poteaux de notre maison comme
J'étais un lézard qui ne connaissait pas d'autre maison
J'ai frappé les murs en jouant au cache-cache
Avec une balle fraîche d'avoir déchiré un autre coffre
Je les ai regardés et leurs armes longues qui sonnaient
Comme des coups durs qui tombent sur les portes de mon cerveau
Je savais que même les larmes ne purifieraient pas leurs âmes souillées
Avec le sang de nos mères et assombri par la fumée de
Cadavres carbonisés des filles qu'ils ont violées et mutilées
Et brûlé.
Donc, quand j'étais fatigué de rouler ma tête
Je me suis retiré du poteau et je me suis assis
Et j'ai donné la balle qui est venu plonger pour me libérer
Un dernier regard long craintif et reconnaissant.

To the One I Miss

Tatah Allen Laika

Banging the bolted doors of peace.
Clanging the heads to reason as a piece.
Clanking the "torn" and opaque drum with ease.
Spanking the "empty" heads to unfreeze.
Damming the dirty tank of mental insalubrity.

Oh, yesterday I said you were unfair.
Today I yearn to harbour half of you.
I genuflect, I thank that adorable epoch.
I weep, I wail, I mourn, I regret being unfair.
Yes, unfair to thee who was tolerant.
Give me a chance to see, feel and taste thee anew.

I know you travelled to show your impact.
But I implore thy indulgence to come back.
I have learned a lesson that you wanted me to.
I'm a fast learner though with my human frailty.
I'm a human, descendant of Adam I'm a sinner.
I yearn to be perfect but perfection not of this world.
Give me a second chance to right the wrongs.
An opportunity once given not to miss again.

So, I wait for your triumphant entry.
Like the one into Jerusalem.
The red carpet, an army of "sinners" awaits thee.
Visibly happy but deeply sorry for their crimes.

We shall rejoice but I am sure you shall weep.
Oh yeah, weep like Christ did.
I know you will when you shall see a Desert.
You will grieve because you left a Paradise.
You will see orphans, widows, widowers, amputees, etc.
But you left the Holy Families.
Please take heart like we have been doing.
So impatient are we, waiting like Vladimir and Estragon did for Godot.
We know you won't delay. We know you are coming soon.
Is it now? Tomorrow? Soon?
Or like a Thief in the Night?
We miss you Mr. PEACE.

Our Hearts Are Heavy

David Chukwudi Njoku

our hearts are so heavy
with words unspoken,
they call us displaced...
and yet no provisions
for us to be fed well
and placed...

is it our fault that
our parents died?
is it our fault that
brought divorce and wars?

we are political tools,
slaves to these rogues,
taken into the forest
and called a chameleon's
name: IDP camp.
some of us barely survive,
some end up in homes
where they are made slaves
while a few end with some
good folks…

whose fault is it:
government, parents
or the society?
i am speaking for my
fellow "displaced..." as they
call us
we hunger all day long,
no good clothing,
not even a good meal
nor proper healthcare.
my case is a little better
because I am with good
foster parents…

is it our fault?
please, come and rescue my
brothers and sisters
in these dilapidated structures…

we are in pain,
we are treated
like we are not humans
even though i am better
with my foster parents
but I feel their pains,

and our hearts are heavy...

La Douleur

Beaton Galafa

Fils
La douleur ne
nous apprend rien
nous nous assoyons et regardons les chiens et les mouches lécher nos blessures
alors que nous attendons impuissants la mort pour nous sauver de nos cavernes
de souffrance, nos frêles cadavres empilés les uns sur les autres
en attendant les sons des massues et les chansons des partis
nous découvrir—pour nous envoyer ou nous ramener à la maison où nous nous
réunirons
avec les morceaux brisés de nos coeurs, et la litière dans les rues en disponibilité
pour une autre élection.

Genocide

Ngam Emmanuel Beyia

My people wear yellow scarfs as you see,
Signed like beasts for extermination
With racial expletives to downgrade me:
"Microbes," "Kaffir," "rats," "good for extinction."

Why do you deny us of our humanity?
Why tag us with disgusting animal names?
Why are my people killed with impunity?
Don't you see how revenge killings crop to avert blame?

You use mob crime as impetus to slaughter.
Your squads, hysteria spreads, armed to murder.
Haven't you heard "ethnic cleansing" in Bosnia?
Haven't you heard of "rotanade" in Algeria?
Targeted killings, mass graves in Ambazonia?

Culture, a bait you use to murder
And want it not called murder!
Rats we're, so you dodge the word "extermination."
Euphemizing your atrocities, you use "purification."
Is this our own beautiful fate in creation?

Whirlpool of downward mass killings,
Vultures fight over cadavers left by zombies
Whose power quest deprive them of humane feelings!
Moderates slaughtered like in horror movies!

Did you know that every genocide
Always comes after countless denials?
That historical facts were all always destroyed
And every report of evidence becomes "alleged?"
Today the guilty dismiss reports as propaganda,
An aching repeat of the demise in Ruanda!
Ceaseless blood scenes keep emptying humanity
Into seas of monstrous depravity.
Only mutual love can restore our dignity.

—16 October 2019

Sceptres without Scruples I, II & III

MD Mbutoh

I – castrated truth

When under the sooth of an
Insane loner's mind, a gun went rampage,
An octogenarian hand in the foliage of Africa was
Quick to pen sincere tears to a maddening
Headsman who has no regard for other races.

When in Paris terror gripped bemused
Souls in the groins and beat pulses like dotting mallards, sympathy rained.
Carcasses have fallen on knocked knees like be-ruffled chickens.
I watched with dismay, African leaders wailing with large tyrannical
Mouths in the funerals of unknown souls under Alien suns—kissing red skulls

But when in the Sambisa little girls are crucified and
Puppetted to sing and recite the songs of hatred,
African sceptres crossed their moseying legs and sip
The blood of their suppressed people in Southern Cameroons
From adorned femurs and sit on sweating Skulls.

II – and the loud silence

When in Mogadishu insanity breathed hatred and bombs
Committed suicide under the scrutiny of a silent bloody sun,
African coronets have gone into coma and dreamed
Of the cries of dying victims in Mamfe and Graffiland beneath
Smiling diadems and royal lances.

When in Buea and Nkambe Deputies have been gassed to
Their ghostly apparitions, sceptres have hidden into the forest
Of Switzerland and rumour has it that Equatorial Guinea
Has become a hideout for killers of freedom & undertakers of free speech.

When old wine convulses young drinkers and makes them dance
On the toes of fire, dyed grey turf rests slackened sinews on the rhythm of
Cadet fury, the Mediterranean regurgitates and belches the flavour
Of mature beef on Italian shores and Mexican forests.

III – and a petal each

A petal each,
It is a lie and the blame game
Sails deep into the ears of the ocean.

A petal each,
And the lies of a tyrant heal
The wounds of trampled souls.

Wounds are hydras with the hair
Of medusa to those who suffered the
Bites of injustice in history.

Petals of blood and they eat their
Own lies on the table of occultism
Whence gallons of blood are wine.

Sceptres vary stupidity too
As selfishness bears petals of blood;
But should you flinch from truth,

You would gather petals of blood!
Dishonest, arrogant authority
Birthed inhabitation & petals of blood you shall drink!

A pig remains a pig even with the finest lining;
Tyrants remain tyrants even with best democracies,
After all, they're sceptres without scruples—it's their nature.

L'Entre-Deux

Josiane Nguimfack

Nous nous révoltons c'est bien beau
We want to make our point of view heard
But how? Is it really the best way?
Montrer qu'on peut kidnapper, violenter et tuer impunément
And swing on social media without the risk of getting caught?
But have we thought about the fallout?
La génération du plus fort est en marche vers la rébellion
Trop de violence dans cette vie déjà niaiseuse
Tired of seeing my country decomposing like shit
Marre de voir le laxisme atteindre son paroxysme
Tired of seeing babies suckled with guns
What is this shit life?
It looks like in a western film
La criminalité frôle le quasi naturel
The world is no longer shocked by anything
A student kills his teacher and it's good
Une autorité gifle un enseignant en plein exercice
Mais il y'a quoi de bien plus normal
The nurse films patients instead of providing care
Au-delà des rancoeurs et des douleurs du passé
Je vous en conjure sauvons notre progéniture
Too much violence punctuates our daily lives
Il y'a en marre. ENOUGH!

Let It Stop, the Crying Fire!

Abraham Gideon Kyari

The crying land unleashes it,
I will grow no plant of yours.
I refuse to take your Red-water.
I will bear no hole for your sake anymore.
Let the crying stick in your milk hand
Stop watering Red-water.
All I need is the uncoloured water.
Let it stop, let love and silent laughter and smile sing.
The begotter, crying out loud with
Whole-sea of sorrow joy.
The begotten, a grown feeble milk lamp.
Why do my youth let the hungry tiger roam the land
And make you clap out rains of fire
At your own giver of life?
Youth, let's dialogue and end the silent cry.
Cast the enchantment of the empty hawk and filthy tiger.
If the crying fire stops, let's stop to sigh
For our lost happy moments.
Let the crying fire stop rather.
Youth, hand the gavel, computer and alphabet.
Brother, we came from same root,
Suck from same nipples,
Wash in same bathroom.
Why has your toy turned a crying fire of blood?
Why are we wrapped in white sheet?
Youth, red and black sheet of souls?
Take off your dirt sheet, put on this with me, blood.
We are begotten for a higher purpose.
Not the evil of the hawk, who gave dirt for peace.
Why does your crying fire tear
On me the Red-water of death?
We should walk and toy around with smiling faces?
Why pain the eye and hate?
Blood, let the crying fire stop.
Let's walk of gold, not that of my own blood.
Cast the dirt of the tiger and hawk.
Let's dove all white.

Il faut enfin la paix

Luc Koffi

Le soleil se lève encore sans le gai vagissement des enfants,
L'odeur âcre du sang innocent monte dans nos gorges,
Les vieillards calcinés, les femmes violées, les enfants décapités,
Sous le regard froid des hypocrites, dans le parfum du cigare et du champagne.
Le soleil se lève encore sous les charniers humains largués aux rapaces,
L'odeur des décombres de victimes enfouies dans les grandes forêts,
L'éducation, la santé et la vie, hélas ont été assassinées,
Sous les blancs regards tendres et doucereux.
Cameroun ! Viens, assois-toi et regarde :
Le rire a fui tes enfants,
L'unité a quitté ta famille,
Reprends donc tes enfants et donne-leur la vie, la paix.
Tends-leur la main et accepte-leur le pardon.
Rends-leur l'amour et la joie.
Viens, assois-toi et regarde :
Tu verras le ciel blanc se réjouir de ton mal sans pitié
Car dans ton sein, ton or et ton pétrole valent mieux que ton amour et ta paix.

The Night

Nnane Ntube

Dog days haunted all,
Lambasted hearts sang dirges
As the pummel fell on us.
Bodies, properties and hopes kaput,
Amortised to ashes.
They, the effigies of the state did these.
It was a pyromaniac night,
The air full of unheard messages
Suspended in the back of tongues
Of canicular sophistries.
Darkness stood before me in mini-skirt,
Soporific skirt,
And my eye lashes bowed
Though I sought asylum in this claw-back skirt,
Stout claws still fell on me.
Etching pains!

Tumultuous Times

Jabulani Ndlovu Mzinyathi

Then you left in a huff
The living was getting rough
The vortex of violence
The raging fiery inferno
Some say you ran away
The fire razing your home
That you had to extinguish
In the still of the night
You left for another country
That country called exile
There to face horrors of rejection
Family ties brutally severed
The turbulence within
Today tumultuous times still
The news from what was home
What still is home to you?
The mind gripped by anxiety
The bags you pack and unpack
Hearing of the fragile peace
Hearing of self-seeking politicians
Your mind in turbulence still
Conflicting stories reverberating
Throwing your mind into a whirlpool
Trying to bridge that gap
The gap between truth and lies
The tumultuous times dog you still
Well you are not alone in this
The tired masses back home wait
Dying in anticipation of respite
Retaining that resilience still
Swallowing that drug called hope
Trying to look back into the future
Yearning for a lustrous future
Wondering whether the trust is misplaced
Wondering whether the leopard changed spots
For the first cut is the deepest
For the cock will always crow
And the dove will always coo
Waiting in anticipation of the good times
When the wounds will heal
When African laughter will resonate
And the world will join in the fun

Je vis sans vie

Baldine Moussa

Des hommes à descendre, nos maisons en cendres
Une pluie de cartouche inonde tout le village
Cette fois-ci ma désespérance a fouiné la mort
La main d'un ami m'a empêché de me descendre
Me faire manger par le feu, devenir son pâturage.

Dans les restes de notre foyer se reposent des corps,
Cramés, sans noms, ni identités, ni quoi que ce soit
A leurs yeux, auront le même statut que les bestiaux,
Sans vie tapissant chaque coin de ce secteur meurtrie
Ils m'ont pris plus qu'une vie, ils ont pris ma voie,

Famille, foi, voisins, un village : un crime de trop !
Dans une forêt dense, sombre, froide et bénie,
Quelques voix vivantes, malades, me parlent ;
Me convainquent de donner espoir à la vie,
Qu'elle mérite aussi une seconde chance,

Que je ne devrais pas faire confiance au trépas
Que rester du côté des morts donnerait victoire,
Aux assassins-pompiers, colportant la tourista
Politique, maquillant des discours garnis de foire,
Quotidiennement afin de berner le peuple
Dans une sorte d'amnésie durant des siècles
Mon fantôme, vivant, hésitant, se doute de tout
Je resterai parmi les morts tant qu'ils seront partout
Ils m'ont tout pris, même mon coeur pour prier
Je vis sans vie ; les leurs me privent de prier.

Why casting slur on your fellowman…?

Wisdom Zachariah

Prodigal Son of Africa?
Your pockets full of graves scattered on the green badge
Refugees lumping the neighbouring IDPs
Reconcile…! Resolve…! And build your nation
For your nooks and crannies know no development
Even your helpers are less and helpless… Only hegemony!
But let scholars rebreed
Resist the mockery of those businessmen, trading your lives…
Separating the goose from the ganda with race, religion and party
Those politicians in flattery and lip-service of propaganda
Destroy the Government!
But Nemesis!
A retributive justice! A seed that germinates!
Oppressed! Speak to the press
Speak on the table… Not through politics of haughty barrels
For against unity, fury subdues the Nation
Repractice the reunification monument…which is…
The Golden star on your National badge
Though wealth, love dignity and peace fell in blood
But under God shall your children be and future see…
The Ivory of Gold and peace!

To You in Ambazonia

Omadang Yowasi

Ambazonia, my Ambazonia
This soil is ripped, raped.
The needless pain unto us.
Where shall we turn to?
Ambazonia, my Ambazonia
Our voices have drowned,
The scarlet ribbon raised.
Who cares where we fall?
Ambazonia, my Ambazonia
You've been hanged!
Your amenities, a ridicule.
You'll walk once again.
To the left to the right, Ambazonia
To bury is to lose forever,
Erased are your footmarks
The time is now, not soon.
Ambazonia, sweet Ambazonia
Listen to the orphans' plea,
Blood shouldn't be in vain,
Clench your fists tighter.

Cartes corporelles et virtuelles

Nsah Mala

Le Chef de mon village trace des cartes sur nos corps.
Sa Majesté est expert en cartographies corporelles.
Comme un dessinateur professionnel,
Il travaille sur les corps tombés en guerre.
Les cadavres victimes sont les tableaux
Sur lesquels il peint les portraits politiques.

Si tu tombes au front contre Boko,
Que tu sois civil ou soldat,
Il va te honorer, parfois avec un deuil national.

Si tu tombes au front dans la zone Anglo,
Son encre peut couler dans plusieurs sens sur le papier.
Si tu es soldat, il te donne des honneurs sans deuil national !
Si tu es civil, c'est le silence qu'il trace, malgré ton sang camerounais !
Si tu es Amba-Boy, c'est une fête nationale, malgré ton sang camerounais !
        Quand tu portes les armes contre l'Etat, Tu perds ta nationalité ?
        A quoi sert donc les reconciliations ?
        Entre dialoguer et faire la guerre, lequel coûte cher ?
        Bonne question pour les cimetières, on nous dirait !

Quand les trains mangent nos villageois
Sur les rails aux cheveux blancs de vieillesse,
Quand les voitures avalent nos villageois
Sur les pistes serpentines remplies de trous,
Le Chef reste muet dans les palais lointains !
Le Chef déguste ses vins dans les hôtels ailleurs
Et ne peut descendre sur le terrain verser les libations !
Mais, il ne tarde jamais d'envoyer ses condoléances
Quand les malheurs frappent les villages d'autruis,

Même des grands malheurs, même des petits malheurs !
C'est ainsi qu'il tisse des belles cartes corporelles.

Sur les ordres du Chef, les experts technologiques
Ont coupé le village en deux.
Sur les claviers, ils ont conjuré l'obscurité technologique,
Divisant le village en deux.
Retraçant ce clivage colonial, ils ont donné raison aux combattants
Qui revendiquent leur liberté sur la base de ces lignes impériales.
Ces lignes que les araignées coloniales ont tracé sur mon Afrique !
Ces traces laissés par des canards blancs en quête d'insectes noires !

Derrière ces cartes virtuelles,
Derrière ces cartes technologiques,
Se cachent les cartes corporelles
Embellies par les corps entassés dans des cours d'eaux
Par les soldats professionnels !
Derrière ces cartes virtuelles,
Derrière ces cartes technologiques,
Se cachent les cartes corporelles
Embellies par les bébés, les maman et les papas brûlés
Par les soldats professionnels !

Sur les ventres des femmes enceintes éventrées dans les hôpitaux,
Les médecins du Chef tracent des cartes corporelles exceptionnelles.
Les trous et les entrails sont des régions et des départements.
Sur les jambes des avocates-activistes comme Michelle Ndoki,
Les policiers du Chef tracent des cartes corporelles adorables.
Les cavités ouvertes par les balles réelles sont des avertissements.
     Des avertissements politiques qui crient :
     On ne remplace jamais un roi Bantou encore en vie !
Sur les visages des politiciens et militants tabassés dans les prisons,
Les geôliers du Chef peignent des cartes corporelles magnifiques.
Les blessures et les ecchymoses sont des délimitations géopolitiques.
     Des délimitations géopolitiques qui nous rappellent
     A qui appartient le pouvoir à jamais, comme au début,
     Maintenant et pour les siècles des siècles,
     Que le reine des cartes corporelles et virtuelles demeure. Amen !

—Aarhus, le 01 août 2019

Cry the Beloved Country

Ngam Emmanuel Beyia

Looking up, I still see skies murky, smoked
By farting dynamites, hired fires from the alien
Ignited by sanctimonious incendiaries
Roasting their own eggs for supper;
Homes, livestock and folks ablaze.
Hills, valleys, brooks burned by dirges.
Crimson waterscape of Ambas Bay
Stands spiritless, awed at land
Pervaded by callous inhumanity,
Ruled by whips and cruel degrees.
Standing still on Epassa Moto's peaks,
I see Sycophants still religiously
Stooping to worship tyranny!
Leeched to sceptre like sticky glued gunk,
Bureaucrats grow bulky and rich,
Sponsoring war for gain and fame;
Masses eclipsed in lies, sacrificial lambs
Weakened by poverty and corruption;
Children out of school caught
In Crossfires of the master's war;
Choked, pressmen's ink goes mild;
Thousands in hellish dungeons gnash their teeth.
Randomly hunted by framed justice,
They're victims for speaking Truth,
Caged incommunicado,
With no right to clemency.
Scourge of genocide rooted in hearts!

Screams of oppressed shrouded
In calculated global conspiracy;
Whistle blowers stand and watch
Men fumigated like pests,
Sepulchred in mass graves;
Blood-thirsty cannibals at work,
Spewing the Hutu animal spirit!
Fate of a graceless bunch
Caught up in dilemma's horn.
Will they stay and be killed
Or will they fight to be free?
Will they escape to fight another day
Or will they die fighting for their freedom?

-17 August 2018

When Will the War Be Over?

David Chukwudi Njoku

When will the war be over?
Here lies my mother.
I am both the nurse
and the doctor.
Everywhere is death –
no farm produce…
no money to fend…
all around are pangs of poverty
launched by the politicians
whom we voted
and the ones who rigged…
How lost are we
in fighting a war
that's been won
by the other camp…?
Many are we in such maladies.
Funny how my parents still
cast their votes
for these double-coated tongues…
When will the war be over?
I mean this ruse of politicians.
When will their gimmicks
and pranks of promises
be over?

Les armes et l'école

Nsah Mala

Ne pas aller à l'école est un sacrifice ultime
Pour acheter la liberté, pour obtenir l'indépendance,
Car l'éducation dans l'esclavage ne vaut rien,
Pensent certains.

Il faut à tout prix que les enfants aillent à l'école
Pour apprendre à vivre ensemble, pour garantir leur avenir,
Malgré que certains vieux ont confisqué cet avenir-là,
Insistent les autres.

Mais la réalité nous guette en face :
Une grenade, une ammunition, ou une balle
Ne distingue pas les écoliers des adultes et des cibles.
Au moins, on n'a pas encore fabriqué les armes intelligentes
Qui distinguent les ennemis des complices et des amis !

Pourquoi ne pas simplement
Déposer les armes dans les deux camps
Pour que les enfants rentrent à l'école ?
La craie ressemble-t-elle à une balle ?
Peut-être les mélodies mélancoliques émises par les armes
Sont des nouveaux hymnes composés pour les écoles de demain.

Seuls le temps et le vent démasqueront l'anus de la poule.
Seuls le temps et le vent dévoileront la nudité de la vérité.
Attendons voir, seulement !
En attendant, vive l'unité sur le sang !
Vivre les termites et les asticots qui se moquent de nous,
Fêtant sur des innombrables cadavres de l'unité !

—*Aarhus, le 17 septembre 2019*

Free at Last

Ngam Emmanuel Beyia

Daily she walked the lane of freedom
T'was rough, tough fighting tyranny in the kingdom
Accepting captivity was according a cursed nativity
Liberty never given, so she fought with all ability

Slave status others simply embraced
Silenced, feeding fat, yet a lot captured
She knew freedom's history was in resistance
So, desire to free land hardened her resilience

After a kangaroo court, interned in a cocoon
Shackled to be silenced by the monsoon;
Torturing chrysalis didn't dampen the spirit
Patiently she waited to resurrect from the pit

Anyone arresting freedom would arrest a ghost
A revolution, a spirit, so many a man did boast,
Announcing it was intangible and invisible,
But, its embers glowed, eternally unquenchable

Butterflies' time awaited, liberty's own time
Miracle of resurrection to occur with bells chime
Cocoon breaking open, for them to fly out triumphant
Tomb's days over, all'll join their dance in songs jubilant

The fetters let loose and their lives bettered
Sunlight of human spirit and dignity restored
All the doors of jails flung widely opened,
At last freedom's feathers will be purchased

–03 September 2019

Bezimbi le Soldat de Plomb

Samy Manga

J'avais besoin de servir un pays
Ils ont écrit mon nom sur le pavé des combattants
J'étais jeune avec un besoin patriotique
Ils m'ont donné une terre avec une étoile
J'avais besoin de liberté
Ils en ont créé une à mon image
À l'aube des conquêtes, ils m'ont dit, tiens, vas-y
J'ai contemplé le regard mou de ma femme
Entendu le coeur lourd de mes enfants
Puis j'ai cajolé le visage de celle qui m'a donné le souffle
J'ai pris quelques effets
Une photographie
Une serviette
Puis un paquet de souvenirs et je suis parti.

Ils ont dit que j'avais un honneur à défendre
J'ai armé mon esprit de haine et de cartouches fantômes
Ils ont trouvé un nom à mon ennemi
Une silhouette au persécuteur de notre nation
Un chapeau, des chaussures, un costume à son aise
Le mal était lui
Le mal était avec lui
Il était la cause
Oui l'autre
C'est bien de lui qu'il s'agit
La gangrène de nos vices
L'absolue torpeur existentielle qu'il fallait rayer
Qu'avait-il fait pour arborer cette fatalité… ?
Là n'était pas le questionnement
Il devait crever, mourir derrière les barreaux de l'exil.

Coûte que coûte
La patrie était en jeu
Elle était en feu
Un drapeau pendu pissait en berne
La sécurité Nationale était le seul but
Sauver un homme, protéger un élu
Le seul tout pour lequel il fallait tuer
Pour lequel il était beau et noble de tuer.

À défaut de l'ennemi, nous avons tiré sur des enfants, tiré sur des hommes et des femmes qu'on ne connaissait pas, à un moment il nous a semblé avoir tiré à bout portant sur l'Amour des gens, mais, un soldat, ça ne pose pas de questions, ça obéit, ils ont dit que c'était la seule façon de semer la Paix, alors, j'ai tiré, durant des jours, durant des semaines, durant des mois, et des années.

Insaisissable, l'ennemi était sans domicile fixe
Il était toi
Il était moi
Il était avec nous
Il était avec eux
Omniprésent, il était partout à la fois, déambulant sur tous les fronts, opposant les révolutionnaires, les nationalistes, les politiciens, les insurgés, et les têtus, il façonnait les esprits, fabriquait des dogmes de colères, ravitaillait le Nord en munitions et le Sud en stratégies.

Un jour en attendant le jour avec une fausse espérance, en attendant la fin de la guerre, l'oreille collée à un poste radiophonique, nous avons dessiné des fleurs et des éléphants pour nos enfants, nous avons soufflé sur les bougies de leurs anniversaires et nous avons ri aux éclats, mais seulement, ces fleurs qu'on avait gravées sur nos casques portaient une triste histoire, un triste collier de sang, une vaine odeur de deuil, une carence de foi paternelle douée d'un amour égoïste.

Nous nous sommes regardés du fond de nos cécités, en quoi est-ce que nos enfants étaient meilleurs que ceux de nos ennemis ? Pourquoi tous ces hommes devaient mourir ? Pourquoi faisions-nous ce travail qui semblait accomplir le rêve d'un autre ? La Nation était peut-être notre seul vrai ennemi, la Nation était peut-être devenue l'ennemi du peuple.

Soudain comme s'ils n'eussent jamais existé quelques secondes avant, sans avoir eu le temps de déserter l'armée, une bombe explosa dans la tanière, mes camarades étaient tous morts, moi aussi d'ailleurs, l'un d'eux tenait encore le stylo qui avait dessiné un ciel à son fils, l'autre saignait du nez tout en regardant son estomac sectionné sur ses genoux, un autre tenant fermement sa mitraillette ravalant sa langue et la sueur de son corps.

Un autre avait le cerveau perforé et la mâchoire en miettes comme si quelques tierces avant la déflagration il avait disposé d'assez de temps pour enfiler un monstrueux masque de cirque.

J'ai enfoncé un bout du drapeau dans le fossé de ma gorge tranchée, autour de moi, il n'y avaitpersonne, aucune de ces personnes qui nous avaient envoyés tuer d'autres personnes à l'autre bout du pays, à l'autre bout du monde
Il n'y avait que nous

Seuls
Rien que nous
Personne à nos côtés
Même pas cette foutue Patrie pour laquelle on avait tant combattu.

Il n'y avait que nous
Seuls avec nous-mêmes
Seuls avec nos ignorances
Seuls avec nos incompétences
Nous étions des corps sans vie, de pauvres soldats qui s'étaient lamentablement trompés d'ennemi, la Nation n'était finalement pas ce qu'on avait cru jusque-là, **un monstre sacré qui broute l'avenir de ses enfants.**

Dawn Shall Come

Ayouba Toure

From the Green Coast- afar
I beheld brethren of the land of unison go asunder
Enfants thrust their mother wombs but with violence
People of one clan serve each other with bullets dating proud.

The green forest is chanting grievances each passing moment
For the ammo has corroded his heart
& he now lives in the hands of vulnerability.

Why have we eaten our cerebrum for breakfast?
And our heart we dine for supper?

For our flag has been shattered into unseen pieces
By revenging wolves
The red lone star has waved us goodbye
& uncertainty sleeps at every doorstep.

I prayed serenity will come like a new-born baby
Just like a rain,
It shall pour its droplets on every thatch hut in our village, Cameroon.

Soon we will see dawn coming from nowhere
& the yellow sun shall come smiling.
At dusk, the moon will shine brighter than never before
& gaiety shall have perpetual nap in our bosom.
Very soon, these prophecies shall come to pass.

Contributors' Bio Notes

Abraham Gideon Kyari was born on 25 May 1995 in Kaduna State, Nigeria. A native speaker of Ham, he did his primary education at Army Children School Dalet Barracks and secondary education at Bethel Baptist High School, all in Kaduna. He later studied history at the Adamawa State College of Education Hong.

Ayouba Toure is a budding poet who writes on the ills of society. He preaches the gospel of African unity. He hails from the land of liberty, Liberia. He's currently a freshman at the University
of Liberia, studying civil engineering.

Balddine Moussa, est un poète né aux iles Comores. Actuellement, il fait son master ès littérature à Zhejiang Normal University en Chine.

Beaton Galafa est un écrivain Malawien. Il a étudié la littérature française à l'Université du Malawi, Chancellor College. Ses oeuvres figurent dans *Stuck in the Library, Transcending the Flame, 300K Anthology, Home/Casa, Betrayal, The Seasons, Empowerment, The Elements, BNAP 2017 Anthology, BNAP 2018 Anthology, Writing Grandmothers, Writing Politics and Knowledge Production, Better Than Starbucks, Love Like Salt Anthology, Literary Shanghai, Mistake House, Fourth & Sycamore, The Blue Tiger Review, The Wagon Magazine, Rejected Lit, Every Writer's Resource, Eunoia Review, The Bombay Review, Nthanda Review, Kalahari Review, The Maynard, Birds Piled Loosely, Atlas and Alice, South 85 Journal* et ailleurs.

David Chukwudi Njoku is a Nigerian faith preacher, writer/poet, songwriter, spoken word artist, social critic, and lover of nature. He has written over 200 poems, and published over 150 poems in Anthologies.

Dr Sadiqullah Khan is a gifted poet of immense insights and creativity. His themes are social, spiritual, and political. Looking at day-to-day living, delving deep into sufferings and joys, he seems to be the voice of the dispossessed and the vast majority of the poor. Yet, his art touches the high mark of existential writing. Unique in style and composition, he appears to lead his own genre. He belongs to Wana, South Waziristan, in Pakistan.

Ekpe Inyang is a Chevening Scholar and author of the award-winning collection of poems titled *Death of Hardship* (2008). He has published eight plays and five collections of poems, with one collection under contract and three ready for publication. Some of his poems have appeared in newspapers, magazines, and anthologies. He has also published a number of scientific articles and textbooks aimed at schools, universities, and the general public. One of such textbooks is *Doing Academic Research* (2017) published by Cambridge Scholars Publishing. His research interests cut across environment, education, culture, and the arts.

Franklin Agogho hails from the Northwest Region of Cameroon. In 2016, he won First Prize in the short story category of the National Creative Writing Contest for Youth organized by the Cameroonian Ministry of Arts and Culture. His writing has been recognized by Global Dialogues USA and published in Anthologies edited by Brittle Paper, Bakwa Magazine, and AfricAvenir. In 2019, he participated in a poetry collaboration titled "Pray for Idai Children: the Hypocrisy of Notre Dame." He holds a Master's degree in International Relations and a Bachelor's degree in English Modern Letters.

Né en 1990 en Côte d'Ivoire, **Gbeada Maxence** est un passionné de plume. Il est auteur de plusieurs textes poétiques dont Morphée et Désespoir. Poète engagé, il dépeint dans son texte les atrocités de la guerre au Cameroun.

Géraldin Mpesse, camerounais polyglotte, est diplômé de l'Ecole Normale Supérieure de Yaoundé (Cameroun). Ses poèmes sont publiés dans plusieurs revues et anthologies en Afrique, Europe, Amérique Latine, notamment : *Antologia Mundial, La papa seguridad alimentaria, Best « New » African Poets 2018 Anthology, AFROpoésie,* entre autres. Actuellement, il est le directeur de publication de *Lepan África Revista.*

Goodenough Mashego is a South African award-winning playwright, poet, filmmaker, writer and author. He has published three volumes of poetry – *Journey with Me, Taste of My Vomit, Just Like Space* Cookies, and one collection of essays – *How to Sink the Black Ball.* Mashego is co-founder of Lepulana Musik, an indigenous language hip-hop label. In 2016 his play *The Last Show* won the Saving Endangered Species (SES) Prize and was staged in Los Angeles, USA. He is the 2016 winner of the coveted Voice of Heritage Golden Shield Award, a South African arts activism prize.

Jabulani Mzinyathi is an ex-teacher, ex-magistrate, human resources practitioner and currently a lawyer with the Zimbabwe law firm Garikayi and Company. He received a diploma for excellence from the Scottish International Open Poetry Contest in 1997. He has published two collections: *Under the Steel Yoke and Righteous Indignation.* His work has been published locally and in international anthologies. Jabulani loves music and strums the acoustic guitar. He loves the arts in general. Many yet-to-be-published works fill his closets. Jabulani vows to keep on writing for as long as he can wield the pen or the computer keyboard.

Josiane Nguimfack est passionnée de l'art en général et du théâtre en particulier. Après plusieurs prestations amateurs au primaire et au secondaire, sa formation professionnelle débute en 2010, dès son entrée à l'Université de Yaoundé I, filière Arts du Spectacle et Cinématographie, où elle obtient en 2018 son master, option production théâtrale. Actuellement, elle continue ses études doctorales à l'Université de Laval (Canada) en études théâtrales (mise en scène). Elle publie en 2014 *Lueur en flamme,* aux Éditions L'Harmattan, et en 2018, elle participe à l'anthologie Best *"New" African Poets 2018 Anthology,* eds. Tendai Rinos Mwanaka et Nsah Mala.

Kile Rash Ike, born in 1993, is a Cameroonian poet and writer. After a lonesome childhood, his desire for poetry started in high school when he began practicing rap music using poetry rhymes. At the university, his passion for poetry became indelible. His poetry skills have earned him two gold medals through his collection of poems titled *A Brother's*

Plea. He believes poetry is the detergent for washing off the dust of our souls. And that all Anglophone Cameroonians need peace, equality, love, and unity. Currently, he is a postgraduate student in the English Department at the University of Buea.

Luc Koffi est un poète et écrivain ivoirien né en 1984. Professeur de lycée, il est doctorant en philosophie, option Histoire des sciences et Epistémologie. Il est co-auteur de l'*Anthologie des meilleurs poètes africains* 2018. Son premier roman intitulé *L'Univers des mooches* paraît en 2019. Son article intitulé « Visit the Populist Nationalism of Donald Trump in the Era of Globalisation » paraît également en 2019 dans la *Revue Africa VS North America, Vol 2.* *Sur les traces du soleil* est son deuxième livre, une pièce de théatre qui est actuellement en cours d'édition.

Mbizo Chirasha is a widely-known poet-activist and performance artist from Zimbabwe, currently living in exile in South Africa. He has curated or initiated many literary projects such as Girl Child Talent Festival, Girl Child Creativity Project, Brave Voices Poetry Journal, Miombo Publishing, the Zimbabwe We Want Poetry Campaign, and Womawords Literary Press. He is the 2019 Poet-in- Residence at the Fictional Café and the 2019 African Fellow for the International Human Rights Art Festival (ihraf.org). Mbizo has been visiting artists in Sweden, Zambia, Ghana, Tanzania, and beyond. His experimental poetry collection, *A Letter to the President,* was published in 2019.

MD Mbutoh is a HOFNA poet laureate who hails from the Northwest Region of Cameroon. He has been guest writer in the Short Story Day Africa Workshop and the Bakwa Creative Writing Workshop at the Goethe Institute, Yaoundé, respectively. He has authored two collections of poems: *Refugee Republic* (2017) and *Dance of the Kangaroos* (2018). His work appears or is forthcoming in magazines, newspapers, and anthologies like Afritondo, Praxis Magazine, Kalahari Review, The Sun (Nigeria), The Guardian Post (Cameroon), and Ashes and Memories (2019). His play *Coastland of Hope* received Special Recommendation from the BBC Radio Play Competition in 2016.

Michael Mwangi Macharia is a prolific poet and literary practitioner who posts verses on a daily basis. He is based in the Rift Valley region in Kenya. He studied at Moi University, Eldoret. His commentaries have appeared in *Saturday Nation* Writers' Forum among other media and were anthologized in EAEP's *Echoes Across the Valley.* He has been active with Miombo Publishing online and engaged as an editor with a private company. He has also nurtured youthful talents with his verses performed in national festivals. Poetry offers him a way of emotional release and expression on pertinent issues afflicting Africa.

Nancy Ndeke is an accomplished poet and a published author of long fiction and poetry from Nairobi, Kenya. She loves nature. Her greatest passion is in reading while at the same time writing poetry.

Ngam Emmanuel Beyia, from Cameroonian, is a teacher, activist, poet, and short story writer. He also advocates for justice and peace. His works feature in many magazines and anthologies across the globe. He has received numerous awards of recognition from Facebook poetry contests. He studied at the University of Yaoundé 1 where he obtained a BA in Bilingual Studies (English and French). He then enrolled at the Higher Teachers Training College (ENS) Yaoundé where he graduated with a diploma in Bilingual Letters (Teaching English and French). Since graduation, he has been teaching French in public high schools in English-speaking Cameroon.

Nnane Ntube hails from the Southwest region of Cameroon. She is a peace advocate, poet and teacher. She uses her poetry to advocate for peace, environmental protection, the eradication of gender-based violence and Human Rights. Her works feature in many international anthologies and magazines. Nnane was a panelist of the 2019 African Writers Conference which took place in Nairobi, Kenya, on the theme "Cultural Stereotypes in African Literature: Rewriting the narratives for the 21st-century Reader." She is committed to empowering young poets.

Nsah Mala est écrivain et poète camerounais et auteur de cinq recueils de poèmes, dont quatre en anglais — *Chaining Freedom* (2012), *Bites of Insanity* (2015), *If You Must Fall Bush* (2016), *CONSTIMOCRAZY: Malafricanising Democracy* (2017) et un en français — Les Pleurs du mal (2019). Écrivant en anglais, en français, et en mbesa, il a remporté des prix littéraires au Cameroun et en France. Ses oeuvres paraissent dans *Tuck Magazine, Kalahari Review, Red Poets, Wales - Cameroon Anthology* (2018), *Redemption Song — Caine Prize Anthology* (2018), *Ashes and Memories - Cendres et mémoires* (2019), parmi d'autres. Il co-dirige plusieurs ouvrages collectifs.

Born in 1992 in Tororo district Eastern Uganda, **Omadang Yowasi** is a Ugandan writer and Police officer. His literary work has appeared in international magazines like *Writers Space Africa,* published by the African Writers Development Trust, in Abuja Nigeria, and Writers Global Movement in Osun State Nigeria. His poem "Live Cheers" was published in Ghana in the AFCON poetry series, and the poem "Jezebel" featured in the maiden edition of *Nalubaale* Review, based in Uganda.

Prince Wogu Richardson Eyong hails from the Southwest region of Cameroon. He is a young writer, poet, social critic, and inspirational speaker. He is the author of *Dark Pains,* a novella published in 2018. He has written several articles, short stories, and poems which have been published in local and international journals. He is presently studying English Modern Letters at the University of Yaoundé 1. His commitment to a healthier and stable society spurred him to engage in writing. He is an advocate of literacy, whole education, and social justice.

Ray Ndebi est écrivain bilingue, traducteur, analyste de créativité littéraire, coach littéraire et promoteur du Livre de Qualité. Il est Camerounais et réside à Yaoundé. Il est l'auteur de *The Last Ghost : Son of Struggle* et a contribué à plusieurs anthologies (poésie, nouvelle). Il dirige plusieurs ateliers (Ecriture, Lecture, Traduction), physiques ou en ligne, publics ou privés, parfois dans des universités comme à Lomé (FESTILARTS) en Avril 2019 ou dans des festivals (FI2L Lomé 2018, FESTAE Dschang 2019, RECAN Yaoundé 2019, PaGya Accra 2019, FI2L Lomé 2019). Sa vie se passe au coeur des mots.

Reagan Ronald Ojok is a Ugandan poet, economist and evaluator. He is a motivational speaker with a strong passion for performance art. His poetic fang searches all corners of societal quagmire, spitting out magical lava of thoughts and imagination on papers. He is a Pan-Africanist who believes in the spirit of Ubuntu.

Rudolf Ngwa Akongoh, born in 1985, is a Cameroonian poet and writer. He had a lonesome and rather introverted childhood. His desire for poetry germinated in secondary school but soon morphed into a passion at the university when he established a link between sounds and the beauty of repetition. In 2017, he published his first collection of poems, *Silhouettes of Dawn,* and is currently on the second, *Ogive of Tears.* He believes poetry is an ideal way of telling the sad stories of the IDPs and refugees of Anglophone Cameroon. He currently lectures English Language at St Jerome University, Douala.

Samuella J. Conteh, from Sierra Leone, West Africa, is a writer, poet, dramatist and motivational speaker. She is a member of the Sierra Leone Writers Forum and Board Member of PEN-SL. She is also Matron and Grand Master of Ceremonies of the International African Writers Association, based in Nigeria, and President of the Sierra Leone Chapter. Her poems feature in several national and international anthologies. She recently received the Award of World Poetic Star from the World Nations Writers Union (WNWU) in Kazakhstan. She is also a member of the Motivational Strips Academy of Literary Excellence and Wisdom (MSALEW).

Né en 1980 au Cameroun, **Samy Manga** est Ecrivain Militant Écopoète. Il révèle son engouement pour les arbres et la création littéraire dès l'âge de 14 ans en produisant son tout premier recueil de poèmes, *Terre de Chez-Moi.* En 2012 il publie *Les Acapella du Bois - Sculptures sur Poésie,* une oeuvre majeur encensée par la critique. Il est promoteur de l'Écopoésie et par ailleurs Président- Fondateur de l'Association des Écopoètes du Cameroun. Il est lauréat d'Épi d'or Festival National des Arts du Cameroun, Prix Poésie Internationale Francophone Cese 47 (édition 2018), et Award American School of Yaoundé.

Star Okpeh is a Nigerian writer and poet, Miombo's Review Princess of African Poetry 2019 and author of *The Dance of Dawn.* Her works have appeared in magazines, journals, anthologies and other platforms. Multiple online award winner for poetry, Star has great interest in music, drama and community service. She is also the 2019 reviewer of the K & L Prize for Literature anthology, volunteer at The African Writer's Development Trust and Christian Faith Homes, Abuja.

Born on 15th September 1987 in the Northwest Region of Cameroon, **Tatah Allen Laika** holds a Bachelor's degree in Bilingual Letters and teaches English and French. His passion for literature, especially poetry, dates as far back as his secondary school days. His works have been published in national and international journals. He believes that the pen alone can help to put an end to the persistent cacophony in the world. This explains why he writes tirelessly. His poems/stories are centered around love, peace, war, unity, and nature. He is currently working on a novel.

Zachariah Wisdom, from Kaduna State, Nigeria, is an undergraduate student of English and Theatre Arts. The native speaker of Ham was born on 07 February 1994. He is a #Generations-for- Peace Advocate and Volunteer.

Z-Ulrich de Dieu, de son vrai nom Ulrich BAKOUMISSA NGOUANI, est né au Congo-Brazzaville le 29 juillet 1992. Il est titulaire d'une licence en Langue et Littérature Françaises et détenteur d'un Master en Langue Française et Textes littéraires (LA.F.TE.L.) obtenus à l'Université Marien Ngouabi. Il est actuellement doctorant et professeur de Français. Il écrit depuis 2018 une thèse de doctorat sur le thème *Innovations paratextuelles et narratives dans le roman français de l'extrême contemporain.* Il est auteur de deux recueils de poèmes : *Vent aux quatre saisons et Les Pas du vent.* Il travaille depuis 2013 dans la promotion des lettres congolaises tout en contribuant aux diverses anthologies.

VITA BOOKS

BOOKS CATALOGUE

THE KENYA SOCIALIST Issue No. 1 Edited by Shiraz Durrani and Kiman Waweru 2019 ISBN 9789966133816 Pages 38	PIO GAMA PINTO: Kenya's Unsung Martyr. 1927 - 1965 Edited by Shiraz Durrani 2018 ISBN 9789966189004 Pages 391	MAU MAU THE REVOLUTIONARY, ANTI-IMPERIALIST FORCE FROM KENYA: 1948-1963 by Shiraz Durrani 2018 ISBN 9789966804020 Pages 154	TRADE UNIONS IN KENYA'S WAR OF INDEPENDENCE by Shiraz Durrani 2018 ISBN 9789966189097 Pages 118
PEOPLE'S RESISTANCE TO COLONIALISM AND IMPERIALISM IN KENYA by Shiraz Durrani 2018 ISBN 9789966114525 Pages 124	KENYA'S WAR OF INDEPENDENCE - Mau Mau and its Legacy of Resistance to Colonialism and Imperialism, 1948-1990 by Shiraz Durrani 2018 ISBN 9789966189011 Pages 450	LIBERATING MINDS, RESTORING KENYAN HISTORY - Anti-Imperialist Resistance by Progressive South Asian Kenyans 1884-1965 by Nazmi Durrani 2017 ISBN 9789966189097 Pages 202	MAKHAN SINGH. A Revolutionary Kenyan Trade Unionist Edited by Shiraz Durrani 2016 ISBN 1 86988613 5 Pages 194
PROGRESSIVE LIBRARIANSHIP Perspectives from Kenya and Britain, 1979-2010 by Shiraz Durrani 2014 ISBN 9781869886202 Pages 446	INFORMATION AND LIBERATION Writings on the Politics of Information and Librarianship by Shiraz Durrani 2008 ISBN 9789966189073 Pages 384	NEVER BE SILENT - Publishing and Imperialism 1884-1963 by Shiraz Durrani 2008 ISBN 9789966189073 Pages 280	KARIMI NDUTHU: A Life in Struggle  1998 ISBN 1-869886-12-7 Pages 100 Only available in Kenya

Vita Books are available in Kenya from the following Bookshops
- Prestige Booksellers, Mama Ngina Street next to 20th Century Cinema
- Bookstop, 2nd floor, Yaya Centre, Argwings Kodhek Road,
- Chania Bookshop, Moi Avenue, Tumaini House, ground floor

Available Worldwide from African Books Collective http://www.africanbookscollective.com/publishers/vita-books

Forthcoming Books

Author/Editor	ISBN	Title
Shiraz Durrani & Kimani Waweru	978-9966-133-11-3	Crimes of Capitalism in Kenya: Massacres, Murders, Detention, Imprisonment, Disappearing and Exiling
Shiraz Durrani	978-1-867886-15-8	Escape from Moneyville: A Short Story for Young People
Nazmi Durrani	978-9966-955-88-3.	Tunakataa! We Say No! Resistance Poems in Kiswahili and English
Shiraz Durrani	978-9966-133-12-0	Two Paths Ahead: The Ideological Struggle for the Liberation of Kenya, 1960-1990
Makhan Singh	978-9966-138-95-8	History of Kenya's Trade Union Movement to 1952. (Reprint)
Makhan Singh	978-9966-955-89-0	Kenya's Trade Unions, 1952-56. (Reprint)
Shiraz Durrani & Kimani Waweru	978-9966-133-81-6	The Kenya Socialist: Issue No. 2

Printed in the United States
By Bookmasters